The Vocal Athlete

Application and Technique for the Hybrid Singer

Second Edition

D0888290

The Vocal Athlete

Application and Technique for the Hybrid Singer

Second Edition

Marci Daniels Rosenberg, BM, MS, CCC-SLP

Wendy D. LeBorgne, PhD, CCC-SLP

PLURAL
PUBLISHING
INC.

5521 Ruffin Road
San Diego, CA 92123

e-mail: information@pluralpublishing.com
Web site: https://www.pluralpublishing.com

Copyright © 2021 by Plural Publishing, Inc.

Typeset in 10.5/13 Garamond by Achorn International
Printed in the United States of America by McNaughton & Gunn, Inc.
22 21 20 19   2 3 4 5

All rights, including that of translation, reserved. No part of this publication may be reproduced, stored in a retrieval system, or transmitted in any form or by any means, electronic, mechanical, recording, or otherwise, including photocopying, recording, taping, Web distribution, or information storage and retrieval systems without the prior written consent of the publisher.

For permission to use material from this text, contact us by
Telephone: (866) 758-7251
Fax: (888) 758-7255
e-mail: permissions@pluralpublishing.com

Every attempt has been made to contact the copyright holders for material originally printed in another source. If any have been inadvertently overlooked, the publishers will gladly make the necessary arrangements at the first opportunity.

ISBN-13: 978-1-63550-164-3
ISBN-10: 1-63550-164-4

Contents

Look for this icon indicating there are related multimedia files available on the companion site.

Foreword

The Vocal Athlete: Application and Technique for the Hybrid Singer is the companion to the newly expanded second edition of the primary text *The Vocal Athlete* (LeBorgne & Rosenberg). This practical and accessible workbook includes a valuable collection of CCM voice exercises including over twenty new exercises to assist voice teachers in training students of all levels. The book advocates scientifically sound, medically healthy singing techniques including warm-up and cooldown exercises, as well as vocal exercises appropriate for each singing genre. Although the exercises are intended for the vocally healthy singer, many of them also are applicable to singers with voice disorders and should prove useful to singing voice specialists. The authors stress an extremely important principle, noting that "a vocal exercise is only effective if the teacher has firmly established the intent and purpose of that exercise for a given student's vocal needs/development/growth and modifies it in the moment as needed."

Rosenberg and LeBorgne's excellent companion book helps teachers understand what they are trying to accomplish with various exercises, helping them concentrate more effectively on each student's progress, rather than on just the completion of an exercise task. The book also includes numerous photos and online access to audio recordings of over fifty of the exercises, providing audible models for exercises that might be difficult to understand from written descriptions.

The Vocal Athlete: Application and Technique for the Hybrid Singer, Second Edition includes additional contributions by an impressive and diverse collection of experts in voice pathology and singing, as well as in other fields such as physical therapy and psychology. Like the first edition, the second edition is grounded in solid science and practical experience. It will be an invaluable addition to the libraries of all singing teachers, speech-language pathologists who work with voice patients, singing voice specialists, and acting voice specialists; and its information is equally valuable for laryngology fellows and laryngologists. Like its companion textbook *The Vocal Athlete*, this workbook will continue to be a classic.

Robert T. Sataloff, MD, DMA, FACS
Professor and Chairman,
Department of Otolaryngology—
Head and Neck Surgery
Senior Associate Dean for
Clinical Academic Specialties
Drexel University College of Medicine
Philadelphia, Pennsylvania
Conductor,
Thomas Jefferson University
Choir Adjunct Professor,
Department of Otolaryngology—
Head and Neck Surgery
Sydney Kimmel Medical College
Thomas Jefferson University
Philadelphia, Pennsylvania

Preface

> hy•brid sing•er(n). Refers to the vocal athlete who is highly skilled performing in multiple vocal styles possessing a solid vocal technique that is responsive, adaptable, and agile in order to meet demands of current and ever-evolving vocal music industry genres.

Voice teachers today are often expected to be skilled in teaching and cultivating multiple vocal styles encompassing classical to pop, musical theater, and more. Yet, many vocal pedagogy training programs do not fully prepare the voice pedagogue to teach multiple vocal styles despite the continued growing need for competent contemporary commercial music (CCM) voice teachers. We conceptualized this book to help bridge a gap in the vocal pedagogy world by compiling a collection of CCM voice exercises for voice teachers of all levels to use as a resource in their studios/practices. Designed to dovetail with its companion singing science, pedagogy, and vocal health textbook, *The Vocal Athlete, Second Edition* (LeBorgne & Rosenberg, 2021), this book contains over 70 CCM voice exercises from some of the most well-respected and sought-after CCM voice experts internationally. Contributors' backgrounds and experiences draw from a variety of arenas from performance psychology and physical therapy to prestigious voice teachers and speech pathologists/singing voice specialists.

How to Use This Book

The exercises presented in this book represent numerous techniques shared by the contributors. We have divided the book into two primary sections. Section I encompasses exercises for the mind and body including mental focus, breathing, alignment and jaw/tongue relaxation exercises. Section II focuses on technical vocal work including vocal warm-up and cool-down, registration, and style-specific exercises. Readers will note that some exercises are applicable in multiple chapters. Although several of the exercises contained are similar to singing voice rehabilitation techniques, the intent of the exercises included in this book is for the *vocally healthy* singer, and none of the exercises should cause vocal strain or discomfort. Further, if a singer or teacher notes onset of new voice difficulties such as voice fatigue, change in quality, or loss of range in the absence of an obvious illness, he or she should seek laryngeal examination from a laryngologist.

In the vocal pedagogy arena, most vocal exercises stem from experiences, personal training, and input from multiple teachers, and many of the exercises are modifications and adaptations from former voice teachers or other methods. The exercises in this book come from voice teachers and speech pathologists/clinical singing voice specialists from varied backgrounds and settings. Although some exercises included in this workbook may seem similar, each contributor brings his or her own unique perspective to their exercise. As with all vocal pedagogy techniques, none of the exercises included have been rigorously scientifically studied for efficacy, but they have proven to be effective empirically through years of experience of the pedagogues who have used them. It is the present authors' belief that there are many ways to approach the same vocal problem or issue. However, a vocal exercise is only effective if the teacher has firmly established the intent and purpose of that exercise for a given student's vocal needs/development/growth and modifies in the moment as needed. It is at this level of understanding that vocal pedagogy becomes an art form in addition to a science. Several of the exercises include either photographs, or audio clips to help augment understanding of how to execute that exercise. Readers are encouraged to continue to explore these exercises beyond what is written on the page or provided as an online resource. We have taken care to relate exercises back to the textbook when applicable to provide the reader with a broader framework for reference and consideration. With a broader context and understanding, teachers are encouraged to play, experiment, modify, and adapt exercises and techniques to suit the specific needs of their student with the physiological knowledge of intended vocal outcome. Additionally, if the exercise ultimately does not yield the intended outcome, it is incumbent upon the teacher to reassess and modify in order to suit the specific needs of the student, for it is the process that is important not a specific exercise.

This workbook comes with video and audio files accessible on a companion website. Look for the icon throughout the book indicating there are multi-media files available for an exercise. See inside front cover of the book for the website address and your access code.

We are endlessly grateful for the contributions of these voice pedagogues, speech pathologists/singing voice specialists, performance psychologists, physical therapists, vocal coaches, and body movement specialists to this book, for without their commitment to CCM pedagogy and willingness to share some of their techniques and methods, this book would not have become a reality.

Acknowledgments

We are grateful for each of our contributing authors for sharing their expertise and wisdom with our readers of this workbook. Your unique contributions have allowed us to compile a book providing the hybrid singer and CCM vocal pedagogue a resource manual of exercises to consider. Thank you all!

—Marci Daniels Rosenberg & Wendy D. LeBorgne

Contributors

Thomas Arduini, BA, MS, CAS Education Administration
Retired Choral Director Yorktown High School
Music Department Coordinator
Yorktown, New York
Chapter 8

Tracy Bourne, PhD, Dip. Dram. Arts (Acting), B.Mus (Voice), M.Mus (Performance)
Singing Teacher and Performer
Ballarat, Australia
Chapter 4

Thomas Francis Burke, III, MS, CCC-SLP
Speech Pathologist
Voice Teacher
Corporate Consultant
Brooklyn, New York
Chapter 5

Joanna Cazden, MFA, MA, CCC-SLP
Voice and Speech Therapist
Cedars-Sinai Medical Center
Los Angeles, California
Chapter 1

J. Austin Collum, MA, CCC-SLP
Clinical Voice Pathologist
The Center for Voice Care and Swallowing Disorders
The Ear, Nose, Throat, and Plastic Surgery Associates
Orlando, Florida
Chapter 5

Starr Cookman, MA, CCC-SLP
Voice and Speech Pathologist
Assistant Professor
University of Connecticut Voice and Speech Clinic
Farmington, Connecticut
Chapter 7

Marya Spring Cordes, MFA
Assistant Professor in Acting/Musical Theater
Department of Theater Dance and Motion Pictures
Founding Acting and Alexander Technique™ Instructor
Musical Theatre/Acting Preparatory Program
Wright State University
Dayton, Ohio
Founding Artistic Director of *The Puzzle: A Festival of New York*
New York, New York
Chapter 2

James Curtis
Speech Language Pathologist
Voice and Swallowing Center—Otolaryngology
University of California San Francisco Medical Center
San Francisco, California
Chapter 7

Benjamin Czarnota, BM, MM
Assistant Professor
Coordinator of Musical theatre Voice Study
University of the Arts
Philadelphia, Pennsylvania
Chapter 8

Marci Daniels Rosenberg, BM, MS, CCC-SLP
Speech-Language Pathologist
Voice and Singing Specialist, Vocal Health Center
Department of Otolaryngology—Laryngology, Rhinology, and General Otolaryngology and Speech-Language Pathology
Michigan Medicine, University of Michigan
Ann Arbor, Michigan
Chapters 1, 5, and 6

Jennifer DeRosa, BFA, MS Ed
Associate Voice Teacher
Tom Burke Studio
Hicksville, New York
Chapter 8

Erin N. Donahue, BM, MA, CCC-SLP
Voice Pathologist
Singing Voice Specialist
Blaine Block Institute for Voice Analysis and
    Rehabilitation
Professional Voice Center of Greater Cincinnati
Cincinnati, Ohio
Chapter 3

Emily Dunn, MS, CCC-SLP
Clinical Voice Pathology
The Center for Voice Care and Swallowing
    Disorders
The Ear, Nose, Throat, and Plastic Surgery Associates
Orlando, Florida
Chapter 5

Matthew Edwards, DMA
Associate Professor of Voice and Voice Pedagogy
Coordinator of Musical Theatre and Voice
Artistic Director of The New CCM (Contemporary
    Commercial Music)
Voice Pedagogy Institute
Shenandoah Conservatory
Shenandoah University
Winchester, Virginia
Chapter 8

Naz Edwards
Educator-Actor-Singer
Founder-Actthroughsong.com
Broadway Veteran
AEA/SAG/AFTRA
Ann Arbor, Michigan
Chapter 8

**Joan Ellison, BM (Voice Performance),
    Masters of Music in Teaching**
Teacher of Popular Voice
Cleveland Institute of Music
Visiting Guest Artist
Cleveland Play House
Case Western Reserve University
Lecturer in Voice
Baldwin Wallace Conservatory
Cleveland, Ohio
Chapter 8

Barbara Fox DeMaio, MM, DMA
Associate Professor of Voice
University of Central Oklahoma
Executive Director, Painted Sky Opera
Edmond, Oklahoma
Chapters 3 and 8

Jeffrey Evans Ramsey, BM
Associate Professor
Berklee College of Music
Boston, Massachusetts
Chapter 8

Walt Fritz, PT
Principal, Foundations in Myofascial Release
    Seminars
Foundations in Myofascial Release Seminar for
    Neck, Voice, and Swallowing Disorders
Rochester, New York
Chapter 4

Marcelle Gauvin
Associate Professor of Music
Berklee College of Music
Boston, Massachusetts
Faculty
CCM Vocal Pedagogy Institute
Winchester, Virginia
Chapter 8

Marina Gilman, MM, MA, CCC-SLP Guild Certified Feldenkrais® Practitioner
Emory Voice Center
Department of Otolaryngology—Head and Neck Surgery Voice Movement Integration
Emory University
Atlanta, Georgia
Chapter 2

Billy Gollner, BA, BMus, MA, CLA
Teacher of Singing
The Urdang Academy
London, United Kingdom
Chapter 7

Renee O. Gottliebson, PhD, CCC-SLP
Clinical Assistant Professor
Department of Speech Pathology and Audiology
Miami University
Oxford, Ohio
Chapter 5

Kathryn Green, DMA
Professor Voice and Voice Pedagogy
Director of Voice Pedagogy Graduate Programs
Director of CCM Vocal Pedagogy Institute
Shenandoah University
Winchester, Virginia
Chapter 7

David Harris, DMA
Co-Founder/Director of VoiceScience Works
Music Director of First Congregational Church of Los Angeles
Composer/Singer/Conductor
Los Angeles, California
Chapter 7

Caroline Helton, DMA
Associate Professor of Music (Voice)
School of Music, Theatre, and Dance
University of Michigan
Ann Arbor, Michigan
Chapters 2 and 5

Bari Hoffman Ruddy, PhD, CCC-SLP
Associate Professor
Department of Communication Sciences and Disorders
University of Central Florida
Orlando, Florida
Director, The Voice Care Center
The Ear, Nose, Throat, and Plastic Surgery Associates
Winter Park, Florida
Chapters 3, 5, and 7

Kelly M. Holst, DMA
Associate Professor of Music (Voice)
Wanda L. Bass School of Music
Oklahoma City University
Oklahoma City, Oklahoma
Chapter 7

Laurel Irene
Soprano and Co-Founder/Director of VoiceScienceWorks
Los Angeles, California
Chapter 7

Maria Cristina A. Jackson-Menaldi, PhD
Speaking and Singing Voice Specialist
Co-Founder, Lakeshore Professional Voice Center
Lakeshore Ear, Nose, and Throat Center, PC
Adjunct, Full Professor, School of Medicine
Department of Otolaryngology
Wayne State University
Detroit, Michigan
Chapter 4

Aaron M. Johnson, MM, PhD, CCC-SLP
New York University Voice Center
Assistant Professor
Department of Otolaryngology—Head and Neck Surgery
New York University School of Medicine
New York, New York
Chapter 7

Joan Lader, MA
Voice Therapist, Teacher, Singing Voice Specialist
The New Studio
New York University
NYSTA, NATS, NYSHLHA, Voice Foundation
New York, New York
Chapter 8

Jonelyn Langenstein, MM, MS, CCC-SLP
Speech-Language Pathologist Singing Voice
    Specialist
Emory Voice Center, Department of Otolaryngology
Atlanta, Georgia
Chapter 6

Wendy D. LeBorgne, PhD, CCC-SLP
Voice Pathologist, Singing Voice Specialist
Director, Blaine Block Institute for Voice Analysis
    and Rehabilitation
Director, The Professional Voice Center of Greater
    Cincinnati
Adjunct Professor
Cincinnati College Conservatory of Music
Cincinnati, Ohio
Chapters 3 and 8

Patricia M. Linhart, BM, MM
Educator Associate Professor of Musical Theatre
    Voice
College Conservatory of Music
University of Cincinnati
Cincinnati, Ohio
Chapter 8

Adam Lloyd, MM, MA, CCC-SLP
Voice Pathologist and Singing Specialist
The Voice Care Center
The Ear, Nose, Throat, and Plastic Surgery Associates
Adjunct Professor of Voice
Rollins College
Winter Park, Florida
Chapters 3 and 7

Jeannette L. LoVetri, NYSTA/NATS, AATS, SVW™
Director, The Voice Workshop
New York, New York
Artist-in-Residence, Baldwin Wallace University
Berea, Ohio
LoVetri Institute for Somatic Voicework™
Member, American Academy of Teachers of
    Singing
Member, The Voice Foundation, Advisory Board
    and Young Student Research Award
Past President, The New York Singing Teachers'
    Association
Chapter 7

Sarah Maines, DMA
Voice Instructor
Singing Voice Specialist
The MAINESTUDIO
Portland, Oregon
Chapters 2 and 7

Robert Marks
Private Vocal Coach
New York, New York
Chapter 8

Katherine McConville, MA, CCC-SLP
Speech-Language Pathologist
Department of Speech-Language Pathology
Michigan Medicine
Chapter 6

Edrie Means Weekly, BME, MM
Co-Founder of CCM Vocal Pedagogy Institute
Associate Professor of Voice and Voice Pedagogy
Musical Theatre and CCM Styles Specialist
Advisory Board, The Voice Foundation
Advisory Board, National Musical Theatre
    Competition, NATS
Shenandoah Conservatory
Winchester, Virginia
Chapter 4

Joan Melton, PhD, ADVS
Emeritus Professor, Theatre
California State University Fullerton
Fullerton, California
Program Director
Once Voice Centre for Integrative Studies
New York, New York
Chapter 3

Jeremy Ryan Mossman, BM, MM, Estill Certified Master Teacher
Assistant Professor
Carthage College
Milwaukee, Wisconsin
Chapter 1

Jennifer C. Muckala, MA, CCC-SLP
Speech-Language Pathologist, Voice Specialist,
    Clinical Faculty
Department of Otolaryngology
Vanderbilt Voice Center
Nashville, Tennessee
Chapter 5

Beverly A. Patton, BM, MA, DMA
Associate Professor
Musical Theatre Singing Specialist
Penn State University School of Theatre
Musical Director
Penn State University Opera Theatre, Penn State
    University School of Music
University Park, Pennsylvania
Chapters 5 and 7

Brian E. Petty, MA, MA, CCC-SLP
Speech-Language Pathologist Singing Voice
    Specialist
The Emory Voice Center
Atlanta, Georgia
Chapters 6 and 7

Lisa Popeil, MFA
Voice Teacher
Vocal Coach Voiceworks®
Sherman Oaks, California
Chapter 7

Suzan Postel
Somatic Bodywork for Singers, Certified Pilates
    Instructor
Founder, The Body Sings℠
Guest Faculty, LoVetri Institute at Baldwin Wallace
    Conservatory
Berea, Ohio
Professional Vocalist
Broadway Veteran singer and dancer
Chapters 2 and 3

Kari Ragan, DMA, Singing Voice Specialist (SVS)
Artist in Residence, Voice, Voice Pedagogy
School of Music, University of Washington
University of Washington, Department of
    Otolaryngology Affilitation, SVS
Seattle, Washington
Chapter 5

Edward Reisert, BM, MS
Choral Director
Fox Lane High School
Bedford Central School District
Bedford, New York
Chapter 8

Amelia A. Rollings, BM, BME, MM, PhD
Assistant Professor of Musical Theatre Voice
Department of Theatre and Dance
Western Kentucky University
Bowling Green, Kentucky
Chapter 6

Michelle Rosen, MM
Adjunct Instructor
NYU Tisch School of Drama
New York, New York
Senior Faculty
LoVetri Institute for Somatic Voicework™
    at Baldwin Wallace University
Senior Faculty
Brooklyn Youth Chorus
Private voice studio
Chapter 7

Stephanie Samaras, MM
Private Vocal Instructor
Assistant Professor
Graduate Center
City University of New York
New York, New York
Adjunct Professor
Montclair State University
Montclair, New Jersey
Chapter 6

Sheri Sanders
Voice Teacher
Vocal Coach
Brooklyn, New York
Audition cuts on http://www.music notes.com
http://www.Rock-the-audition.com
Chapter 8

Mary Saunders Barton, MA
Retired Professor of Voice
Former Head of Voice and Graduate Voice
    Pedagogy for Musical Theatre
Penn State University
University Park, Pennsylvania
Chapters 6 and 7

Sarah L. Schneider, MS, CCC-SLP
Speech Language Pathology Director
UCSF Voice and Swallowing Center
Department of Otolaryngology—Head and Neck
    Surgery
University of California San Francisco
San Francisco, California
Chapters 2 and 7

Martin L. Spencer, MA, CCC-SLP
Speech Pathologist
Singing Voice Specialist
The Voice Center at Ohio ENT
Columbus, Ohio
Chapters 1 and 7

Norman Spivey, BM, MM, DMA
Professor of Voice and Voice Pedagogy
Penn State University
State College, Pennsylvania
Chapters 5, 7, and 8

Robert C. Sussuma, MMus, GCFP
http://www.robertsussuma.com
New York, New York
Chapters 1 and 2

Miriam van Mersbergen, PhD, CCC-SLP
Assistant Professor
Northern Illinois University
DeKalb, Illinois
Chapter 4

Jill Vonderhaar Nader, PT
Physical Therapist
Prehab Pilates & Physical Therapy, LLC
Cincinnati, Ohio
Chapter 2

Barbara J. Walker, PhD
Performance Psychologist
Center for Human Performance
Cincinnati, Ohio
Chapter 1

**Catherine A. Walker, BM, MM, Estill Certified
    Master Trainer**
Associate Professor of Musical Theatre
School of Music, Theatre, and Dance
University of Michigan
Music Director, Vocal Coach, Clinician
Founder-Explore the Voice, LLC
Explorethevoice.com
Ann Arbor, Michigan
Chapter 4

Ann Evans Watson
Assistant Professor of Musical Theatre
School of Music, Theatre, and Dance
University of Michigan
AEA, MTEA, NATS, PAVA, VASTA
Ann Arbor, Michigan
Chapter 7

Chris York, BS in (Choral) MusEd
Adjunct Professor
Musical Theatre Department
Pace University
Chris York Voice Studio
New York, New York
Chapter 8

SECTION I

Preparing the Singer's Mind and Body

Introduction and Overview

Given the physical demands of many Contemporary Commercial Music (CCM) styles, this section includes exercises that help provide the foundation for efficient performance. The exercises included in this section address the singer (mentally and physically) as a whole. We have included exercises to promote mental focus and centering as well as for posture, alignment, and breathing. Additionally, stretch and relaxation exercises for jaw and tongue are provided in this section.

Chapter 1: Exercises for Mental Focus

Chapter 1 begins with a variety of exercises designed to promote mental focus and centering. Dr. Barbara Walker (performance psychologist) provides a guided meditation to center the breath and clear the mind. This exercise can be useful to increase mental focus and reduce performance anxiety, allowing the performer to reduce apprehension and feel mentally prepared for performance. Robert Sussuma takes the reader through a voice scan exercise in order to increase the singer's awareness and kinesthetic feedback of his or her instrument prior to active voice use or performance. This exercise may be useful for singers who are kinesthetically "blocked" with reduced awareness of what they are sensing and experiencing when singing. He also presents a Feldenkrais-based lesson on

reorganizing the vocal tract. Joanna Cazden's exercise also promotes self-discovery of the voice, but with a unique intention. Her exercise encourages creation of a dialogue with your voice to explore feelings and emotions about your vocal history with the intention of moving past vocal negativity and frustration, allowing the singer to move toward a healthier vocal viewpoint. This type of exercise can be useful for singers who currently have or are having vocal issues or injury, as it gives the singer a method to verbalize and express fears and emotions associated with singing, while facilitating a process of reestablishing a level of trust with the vocal instrument. Jeremy Mossman's vocal exploration exercise provides an enjoyable arena for a singer to explore various qualities of vocal sounds outside of the context of singing. This exercise has usefulness from a cross-training perspective allowing for the exploration of a variety of vocal colors and nuances that can be drawn upon for performance. Martin Spencer introduces several variations of a mental focus and breathing exercise including a group mental focus exercise to connect and synchronize multiple people through movement and breath. He encourages this exercise as a means to unify and optimize the ensemble dynamic. Finally, the Scale of Vocal Effort (SoVE) rating scale described by Marci Rosenberg is designed to heighten the singer's awareness of the level of baseline perceived vocal effort expended for various vocal tasks. The intention of this exercise is to increase awareness of vocal effort and establish a consistent internal scale allowing the singer to self-monitor for subtle changes in vocal effort. Given the variety of settings and environments the vocal athlete performs in, this is a useful tool for singers to internally gauge possible vocal issues before they become problematic over a longer period of time.

Chapter 2: Physical Stretches and Alignment

As singing is a task involving the entire body, Chapter 2 includes a collection of exercises designed to stretch, release, and align the body. This chapter begins with Sarah Schneider's exercise using body movement to draw attention away from areas of tension, creating a "constructive distraction" in order to free vocal sound. Marya Cordes has provided an Alexander-based stretch, movement, and vocalization exercise to promote fluidity throughout the body in preparation for singing. Marina Gilman's two Feldenkrais-based exercises dovetail nicely to balance the head and release the neck and shoulders while singing. Dr. Caroline Helton's "Climbing the Ladder" exercise is used to open the torso and rib cage. Physical therapist Jill Nader's exercise provides a set of stretches and myofascial release techniques for the upper body, serving to both improve posture and increase mobility and range of motion of the rib cage, chest, and upper back. Suzan Postel describes a posture and alignment exercise to neutralize posture and connect the body to the breath. Dr. Sarah Maines adds to these by providing an exercise promoting stretch and freedom in the lower back designed specifically for vocal athletes.

Chapter 3: Stretches and Exercises for Breathing

Although breathing is incorporated into several of the exercises throughout this book, Chapter 3 includes a handful of specific breathing exercises for the vocal athlete. Erin Donahue and Dr. Wendy LeBorgne provide a set of exercises designed to prepare the respiratory system through chest and abdominal stretches and contractions of the respiratory muscles. Dr. Joan

Melton describes two techniques to free the abdominal muscles and connect the voice to the body. Dr. Barbara Fox DeMaio provides a specialized exercise for building breath stamina in the ageing voice. Dr. Bari Hoffman and Adam Lloyd provide a stylized breathing exercise for vocalists who engage in vocal percussion. This exercise trains coordination and agility needed for this unique CCM skill.

Chapter 4: Stretching and Relaxation for Jaw and Tongue

Because the jaw and tongue can be problematic with various CCM vocal styles, we have included a chapter specifically addressing issues related to jaw and tongue tension release. The first two exercises are provided by Dr. Miriam van Mersbergen. The first exercise is composed of four individual exercises to stretch and relax the four primary muscles of the jaw. Her second exercise addresses the relationship between the back of the tongue and the jaw. Dr. van Mersbergen has also provided guidelines to promote a healthy jaw. Physical therapist Walt Fritz has provided a self-treatment protocol for the jaw. Dr. Christina Jackson-Menaldi provides an exercise combining phonation with base of tongue release. Finally, Tracy Bourne adds another base of tongue release exercise with vocalizations on both staccato and legato patterns.

The exercises provided in this section have relevance for numerous singing styles. They can be used as part of an initial preparation to sing, as well as, during active training, to relax muscles, realign posture, and recalibrate as needed. Singers may discover that what is needed for their body will vary from day to day and role to role. Furthermore, alignment and posture, and general musculoskeletal integrity, can be impacted by a variety of factors such as physicality of a role or even a cumbersome headpiece. The importance of tuning into one's body and psyche to determine what is needed is a vital component of the vocal training regimen, and this practice should be established early in the vocal training regimen

1

Exercises for Mental Focus

Centering the Breath

Barbara J. Walker

Purpose of Exercise

■ To encourage relaxation of the vocal tract
■ To create whole-body relaxation and clear the mind from performance anxiety on cue
■ To allow one to feel in control of his/her body and mind before and during performance, allowing for optimal performance

Origin of Exercise

This exercise is based on diaphragmatic breathing, which is a well-known exercise that Zen masters and spiritual leaders have been using for centuries, and psychologists and yoga instructors for decades. Focusing on the breath allows one to be aware of and have the capacity to take control of one's mind and body. Utilizing cue words and phrases is based in cognitive psychology.

Overview of Exercise

When singers are experiencing stress or performance anxiety, it is usually as a result of negative or anxious thoughts or images about their performance rather than an actual threat or emergency. This reaction may occur after there has been an error at a previous performance or if they have just recovered from an injury, and now they may be feeling anxious that they will not be able to perform optimally. Regardless, their body reacts from these thoughts as if a true emergency were occurring, a fight or flight response. From this reaction, which is driven from a conscious or subconscious thought or image in their mind, their breathing may naturally become shallow and rapid. A vicious cycle then begins, and the singer may also experience the physiological symptoms of an increased heart rate, sweating, muscle tension, decreased oxygen intake, dry mouth, and a sudden loss of energy or feelings of fatigue. Mentally, they may experience worry, feeling overwhelmed and out of control, as well as a loss of concentration (sometimes losing track of where they were in a song or forgetting words). Behaviorally, this may cause them to sing more quickly and/or have a disrupted/broken voice. All of these symptoms can be triggered from a single anxious thought or image.

To ward off any anxiety, in additional to being prepared, mentally and physically for their performance, singers visualizing themselves performing well is also very helpful. Implementing this simple-centered breathing technique at the right time will keep the stress symptoms at bay and will also allow one to recover quickly if any of the above anxiety symptoms develop.

Exercise

When first learning this exercise, it is best to find a quiet environment and a place where you feel comfortable closing your eyes. After the exercise is mastered, it can be accomplished in any environment.

1. You can begin learning this exercise either lying down on your back or simply sitting up in a chair. Begin by placing one hand on your upper chest and the other just below the rib cage. This will allow you to feel the diaphragm move as you breathe.
2. Breathe in slowly through the nose (if possible), so that the stomach moves out against the hand. The hand on the chest should remain as still as possible.
3. Tighten the stomach muscles, letting them fall inward as you exhale through the mouth.
4. As you feel comfortable with the rhythm of the breath, visualize your chest and heart muscles loosening and opening up and visualize your breath coming up and down your chest smoothly and easily.
5. Silently to yourself, count the number of seconds it takes you to inhale, and then make it equal with your exhale. Example: Inhale 1, 2, 3, 4, 5, and then Exhale 1, 2, 3, 4, 5. If you find yourself having any thoughts other than counting going through your mind, count as loudly as you need to inside your mind, allowing any other thoughts to dissipate.

How Often Should I Practice This Exercise?

At first, practice this exercise 5 to 10 minutes about three to four times per day to master the breath. A great time to practice this exercise is at nighttime just as you are going to bed. Once the breath is mastered, implement the breath about 30 minutes prior to a performance or just before you typically begin to feel any anxiety symptoms.

---

6. After you have become fluid with your breathing and counting, you will experience a specific feeling state. What words best describe how you feel: Peaceful? Calm? Relaxed? Quiet? Clear? Ready? Energized? Identify two words that you feel when you breathe and relate that to how you feel when you perform (for example: Confident and Clear; Focused and Relaxed).
7. Whenever a performance is drawing near or if you begin to experience any anxiety symptoms, I suggest repeating these cue words to yourself along with the breath or simply begin the breath along with the counting. With practice, even with just a couple of breaths, this technique will allow you to override and avert any stressful or anxious feelings you may have.

The Voice Scan

Robert Sussuma

Purpose of Exercise

The purpose of this scan is to bring one's awareness to the sensations of the vocal mechanism at rest in preparation for sound and movement. By paying close attention to these sensations before and after singing, we are better able to know our instrument and track the many changes that occur along the way, allowing us to move and sing with more accuracy and clarity of intention.

Origin of Exercise

In the Feldenkrais method, almost every lesson begins with a body scan. The purpose of the scan is to notice how we sense ourselves and what we are aware of BEFORE we do a lesson (or exercise) so that when we do, and things change, we can compare the changes to what we sensed in the beginning of the lesson.

One of Dr. Moshe Feldenkrais' most famous utterances was: "When you know what you are doing, you can do what you want!" This is a provocative statement. Do we really know what we are doing as singers, or otherwise? And, if we don't really know what we are doing, how can we do what we want—especially with our voice?

Overview of Exercise

The Voice Scan will systematically guide you through sensing your vocal apparatus, so that you can become more and more aware of the background sensations connected to your voice. This will form the sensory foundation for all of the intricate movements associated with each sound you can and will make. As this sense grows, one can more easily move away from just listening to the sound or relying on others to know what one is doing!

Exercise

Lie on your back. Sense your contact with the floor. Notice: your heels, your legs, your pelvis, your lower and upper back, your ribs, your shoulders and arms, your neck and head. Which parts feel heavier or lighter? How is your right side different from your left?

Bring your awareness to your face. Notice the expression. How soft are your eyes, your cheeks, your lips?

Bring your awareness to your jaw. How heavy is your jaw? How big is it? How does your jaw connect to your skull?

Leave that and now, naturally, without doing anything special, begin to pay attention to your breathing: the timing, the shape, the movement as you inhale and exhale.

Now, with your mouth closed, breathe through your nose and ask yourself, <u>how does the air get from the nostrils to the lungs?</u>

How much of your airway can you actually sense as you inhale and exhale?

Which parts are clear to you, which parts are murky or confusing?

Which parts don't even seem to be there at all?

(I have found that most people have a clear sense of the air passing through their nostrils and may even clearly feel the air in the back of the mouth, but cannot sense anything from the back of the tongue to the lungs.)

Using your sensory imagination, spend several minutes attending to your sensations in the following areas:

1. *The nostrils to the back of the nasal cavity*: How deep is the cavity? How wide? How quickly is the air moving? What is the temperature of the air? What do your nasal passages look and feel like?
2. *The soft palate*: Sense how the air goes over and behind the soft palate to reach the back of the mouth. What does your soft palate look like?
3. *Behind the tongue*: Sense how the air passes behind the tongue on its way to your throat. How much space is there behind your tongue? Where is the bottom of the back of your tongue?
4. *Into the throat and larynx*: As the air passes through your larynx, it passes through your vocal folds. Where are your vocal folds? What is your sense of your throat as the air passes through it? Notice how it changes shape as you inhale and exhale.
5. *Down to the lungs*: Where does the larynx end and the trachea begin? How does the air get from the single tube of the trachea to both lungs? How does the air fill your lungs? How do your ribs and diaphragm move?

When you have finished sensing the areas above, return to the original question: <u>How does the air get from your nostrils to your lungs?</u> What is your sense now?

Notice your contact with the floor now. How may it have changed as a result of this scanning process?

Slowly roll to your side and sit. Stand. Walk. How do you feel now? What are you most aware of? What is your sense of your breathing now?

Sing something. How has the scan changed your sense of yourself while singing? Has it changed your singing? How might your singing be different as a result of this scan?

Dialogue with Your Voice

Joanna Cazden

Purpose of Exercise

- To understand your vocal history at the level of the feeling-body
- To move from frustration or anger at your limits toward compassion for yourself and your vocal needs
- To improve self-care and healthy-voice practices by cooperating with your voice

Origin of Exercise

I developed this out of varied experiences with role play, psycho-synthesis, peer counseling, and the Gestalt therapy practice of two-chair self-dialogue. (In this case a partner occupies the second chair and participates in the dialogue and in any following discussion.) At its core, the exercise stems from my personal belief that the vocal cords are always trying to accomplish what we ask of them. Whether robust, fragile, ill, overused, or at peak performance, they are absolutely loyal and they want to do their best.

Overview of Exercise

This is a self-discovery exercise that involves both writing and talking. The process can be used at any time, but it will be more intense, and possibly more conflicted, if used during a time of acute vocal strain, rather than if you are reflecting on a past experience.

Requirements are a private space where you and a supportive friend can concentrate without interruption for about 30 minutes, and writing materials of your choice. It is recommended that your partner in the exercise be a peer, rather than a teacher, parent, or other authority figure.

Exercise

Preparation

This can be done in advance, without your partner present. (If present, the partner should sit quietly, practicing slow quiet breathing, silent prayer, or any other technique that helps the partner to be ready to support your exploration. During discussion at the end, the listening partner should avoid judging, problem solving, or advice and simply support your discovery process.)

1. Choose an episode in your life when your voice was especially important in your life or identity. Examples: your preparation period for a big audition; a life-changing decision you made regarding your singing or career development; a period of illness or vocal struggle; or a time of adjustment to a new level of success. You can repeat the exercise some other time for other key moments, or even develop a complete "vocal biography" this way. For now, pick ONE episode to look into.
2. Write a letter to your voice, describing this event in personal terms and addressing the voice as "You." Write down what happened, and your feelings as it happened. Tell your voice how "it" did or did not fulfill what you wanted. Keep your language simple and direct, rather than intellectual; and use short sentences to state your feelings rather than analyzing them.

Dialogue

1. Read the letter to your partner, all the way through, in a dry or matter-of-fact manner, so that you are both clear on what happened.
2. Read the first sentence, and pause. *Your partner takes the role of your vocal cords or vocal instrument and repeats the sentence back with reversed*

pronouns. Continue in this way to the end of the story. Pause and reflect.

3. Ask your partner (still in the role of your voice) how she/he feels about the episode. Listen and reflect on those feelings and on how you might become an even better partner to your own vocal instrument.

Example A

Writer:"I had a big solo in that high school show, and I was afraid you would crack."

Partner:"*You had a big solo in that high school show, and you were afraid I would crack.*"

. . . .

Partner's response at the end of story:"*You know, I didn't want to let you down. I was scared too. But I came through for you, didn't I?*"

Reflection:"Yes, you came through, and I'm grateful. Maybe if I'd been less freaked out, you could have relaxed and sung more easily."

Example B

Writer:"I passed the college audition, and you were so great I even got a scholarship!"

Partner: "*You passed the college audition, and I was so great you even got a scholarship!*"

. . . .

Partner's response at the end of story:"*I love that I got you your scholarship! I was proud for both of us! But then you got busy with moving and everything, and it was weeks before we really sang again.*"

Reflection:"You did a big thing for me. Maybe I could have treated you to a steam treatment before those cocktails to celebrate! I'm grateful I have you."

1. If there is time and your partner is also a singer, you can switch roles and repeat the exercise, to dialogue about the partner's voice. Before you leave the space, make a conscious transition to your normal roles. Confirm that everything you discussed

stays private, and thank your partner for her/his support.

Your Voice in Real Life: A Vocal Exploration Through Laughing and Crying

Jeremy Ryan Mossman

Purpose of Exercise

To discover valuable qualities of vocal sounds found in nonsinging contexts.

Origin of Exercise

Every voice is capable of accomplishing the technical demands of any vocal aesthetic, no matter how opposing some may seem. We all have the same muscles after all—however, we may have only explored a fraction of these possibilities while singing. The Estill model for voice has aimed to answer many questions about the behaviors in and around the larynx during various vocal tasks. In order to understand some of these behaviors, the Estill model looks to how the voice operates in contexts other than singing. Daily vocal usage often encompasses a far broader palette of vocal colors and may contain crucial details for crossing over into different singing styles and discovering for more aesthetic options.

Overview of Exercise

Laughing and crying can be emotional opposites, but sometimes one attracts the other and they become hard to distinguish from one another. When we take away the actual real-life impulse to laugh or cry but maintain the genuine sounds and feelings, we may be able to evaluate perceptual similarities and differences between them. I hope you are able to sense through this exploration a very important feature in healthy singing: the open throat.

This exploration requires nothing more than curiosity to investigate what your voice may already know but hasn't applied in song. It can also be used as a terrific warm-up for your voice, body, brain, and soul.

Exercise

Exploration

1. Laugh. Cry. What did you notice?
2. Find as many variations as you can and qualify each with a name (belly laugh, chipmunk laugh, whiny baby cry, sob, etc.).
3. Evaluate variables of each:

Throat space	Larynx position	Resistance versus airflow
Mouth shape	Support sensations	Activity in the body
Head and neck position	Loudness	Bright/dark
Sensations of placement	Vowel attraction	Amount of breath
Onset (aspirate/ glottal/smooth)		

4. Examine these bursts of sound energy a little further. Can they be sustained? (Make sure you monitor all the variables for consistency of effort.) Can you use them as glides throughout your range? What are other vowels like? Can they have vibrato?!

It's fascinating to recognize that there are indeed common variables across many different laughs and cries. Are your cheeks lifted? How similar is the action in your abdomen? Where do you feel your soft palate? What is your in-breath like? Every laugh and cry on your list has a value in performance. When and where are personal choices, although investigate this idea: Is it possible that the biggest laugh may be akin to belting, whereas the more extreme the cry, the more you are preparing for classical sounds?

It has been documented that voice is governed by both hemispheres of the brain: singing in the right

hemisphere, speaking in the left. The hemispheres are in constant communication and balance each other out. Removing artistry from vocalizing and systematically working with sounds coordinated by the left hemisphere will grow the possibilities available in the right, where you're artistic. Let the left hemisphere teach the right, reduce risk, remove limitations, and really discover what your voice will do. Your homework: Interview your voice in various settings and discover what it already knows!

Mental Focus and Vocal Preparation

Martin L. Spencer

Purpose of Exercise

- To focus on breathing as preparation for relaxed vocal and physical release
- To compellingly transition from the wings to the stage

Origin of Exercise

I was introduced to this mode of this performance preparation by an instructor in the Music Theater Studio Ensemble at the Banff School of Fine Arts in the early 1980s. Under his guidance, our ensemble of artists grew into a tightly knit rehearsing and performing unit.

Exercise

Variation I

Songs are borne on the wings of breath. Relaxed control of breathing is the essential ingredient of phonatory ease and emotional release. However, habitual respiratory tensions such as inspiratory thoracic hyperelevation may sympathetically tense laryngeal musculature and induce overly muscular belting. Therefore, a short period of isolated focus on the breathing mechanism, prior to engaging phonation, may yield freer vocal dividends.

Relaxed "lower abdominal breathing" may be considered a spiritual act. Through physical isolation, it serves as a meditative portal to a powerful awareness of the self in the moment. In theater training and performance, it is essential to engage the authentic emotional self, which is obscured by intellectualizing ego. Within the true self lies the ritualized healing power of theater, as well as artistry.

A holistically minded clinician or teacher may guide a singer to new heights of emotional release. The explosive power contained within great lyrics may be realized through an initial preparation of supine positioning/spinal lengthening and graduated musculoskeletal release. From this relaxed state, teacher-prompted, auto-suggestive implantation of single lines of verse or text may inspire more authentic performer declamation. Across many sessions, trust is built between the teacher and the singer, with deeper revelation of the lyricist's or playwright's message.

Simple stretching movements are also an ideal place to inculcate deep breathing. Integration of breathing awareness into Tai Chi and yoga-based movement patterns is an ideal way to prepare for the immediate transition from off-stage to on-stage awareness. Energy flow and consciousness must be directed outward; this results in compelling performance in which the singer is the servant of both the drama and the audience. Inwardly anxious reflection results in over-intellectualization and loss of empathic connection to other performers . . . and the audience.

Variation II

A novel expansion of a singer's mental preparation for performance is to engage other cast mates so that mental and physical foci are synchronized for optimal ensemble dynamic. The exercise started with the performers standing in a circle. One performer held a light plastic ball, typically found in children's sections of department stores. The performer would toss the ball to another performer in the circle. The ball release was accompanied with gently springing movement of the body and legs. The cast mate would catch the ball in the physical and emotional spirit in which the ball was lofted. Indeed, the whole ensemble started to synchronize to each toss and catch. It made no difference to whom the ball would be directed next, as all were synchronized to its movement across or around the circle. The tosser could control the changing energy of the moment by slowing or quickening the movement dialogue. Daily practice of the exercise resulted in greater unison, and greater ensemble performance inevitably ensued on stage. The ball exercise increased in complexity across time. Looking back, I think that we could have vocalized sighs with each release. What a great way to free both the voice and the body!

Scale of Vocal Effort

Marci Daniels Rosenberg

Purpose of Exercise

The purpose of this exercise is to allow the singer to establish a consistent, internal kinesthetic scale of perceived vocal effort during singing in order to monitor for changes in voice functioning in various settings (training, performing, etc.).

Origin of Exercise

This exercise stems from working with injured singers. Often, onset of vocal difficulty is associated with a change in voice production, or voice demand resulting in either increased voice use or increased effort. However, singers are not always fully aware of possible contributing factors. Having a consistent internal rating system will allow the singer to better troubleshoot early signs of fatigue and possible difficulties.

Overview of Exercise

The exercise is very basic. It simply involves asking the singer regularly to rate, on a scale of 0 to 10, the level of perceived vocal effort. A 0 is absolutely no effort, and a rating of 10 is extreme effort with excessive strain and even discomfort. Sometimes probing is needed in order for singers to differentiate between mental effort and physical effort. Mental effort refers in part to effort that is not physical, such as feeling like they have to really "focus and think" about their voice production task, or feeling discouraged or unhappy about the sound they are producing. Although this type of effort is often important to be aware of and acknowledge, it is not to be confused with physical effort. Physical effort refers specifically to effort sensed somewhere in the body when singing. Over time, the singer should be able to discern specific areas of effort such as effort in the abdominal musculature, versus effort in the laryngeal region or jaw. This level of awareness will allow the singer and teacher to better troubleshoot issues when they arise by adding specific exercises to counter perceived areas of tension. Additionally, it will help the singer generally gauge his or her current vocal status. For example, if a singer perceives a new onset of vocal effort where not previously experienced, he or she should consider several possible explanations, including recent voice use, hydration, or possible onset of illness. Another parameter to consider as a possible contributing factor to increased perceived effort is change in level of amplification or sound. Although we may not think of this as an issue, something as simple as a new sound engineer who has altered amplification settings, or fellow instrumentalists increasing the volume of their instruments during performance, could result in the singer unknowingly compensating and increasing vocal effort.

The goal of this exercise is not necessarily to get every vocal production to be at a certain level (i.e., level 2 or 3), because we know physiologically that certain songs and vocal tasks will simply require more effort to produce. Rather, the goal is for singers to become well informed as to what their expected effort is for various vocal tasks and settings. Singers who are very familiar with their own variations in voice production are better armed to identify and troubleshoot possible issues before they become problematic.

Exercise

■ Have the student complete a given vocal task such as a scale or section of a song.
■ Ask the student to rate the level of perceived vocal (physical) effort for that task. There is no right answer, rather this is the student's process of establishing what feels easy versus effortful. Half steps can be used (i.e., 3.5).
■ If students are visual learners, have them use the grid below to mark perceived effort.
■ If students rate level of effort as high (above 6.0), ask them if they can discern where they perceive this effort (larynx, jaw, abdomen, neck, etc.).
■ Ask students to repeat the task and see if they can sing it again one step lower on the effort scale. Have students reflect again on the level of effort.
■ If needed, provide an exercise(s) to help address the area of perceived effort and continue to check in periodically with the students for the SoVE rating.

SoVE Rating

0	1	2	3	4	5	6	7	8	9	10
No effort			Medium			High			Extreme	

Notes

2

Physical Stretches and Alignment

Body Movement to Achieve Vocal Freedom

Sarah L. Schneider

Purpose of Exercise

- To use body movement to refocus areas of tension away from the vocal mechanism/voice production
- Provide muscle confusion during vocalization to allow for increased vocal ease
- Increase multitasking during voice production to provide a constructive distraction
- To indirectly improve coordination of respiration, phonation, and resonance

Origin of Exercise

This series of physical body movements is an adaptation of exercises I have learned over the years in acting and singing workshops. In exercise physiology, there is a term called *muscle confusion*, simply put, the muscles in the body adjust to certain stressors or routines and begin to plateau, or find a new homeostasis. When we introduce a variable exercise routine and new movement, then muscle confusion takes place. This may be what takes place when a specific body movement is paired with vocalization in someone with muscle tension dysphonia and/or inefficient voice use patterns. Still, the exact reasons specific body movements are helpful are not fully understood. However, during the vocal rehabilitation process, these exercises often aid in establishing a new sense of awareness and lead to increased vocal freedom.

Overview of Exercise

Three (four) different body movements targeting three (four) different areas of the body will be introduced. These are to be paired with vocalization, typically a voice exercise, for example, tongue-out trills, flow phonation, and resonant voice exercises. The goal is to maximize vocal ease by refocusing tension, allow for more coordinated breathing and phonation, and increase the ease of finding forward resonance. Each of the exercises can be completed in isolation or in combination with each other.

Exercise

I. Head Turn

1. In a seated or standing position, find a neutral posture with the shoulders above the hips and the ears above the shoulders. Begin vocalization.

2. During vocalization initiate a head turn—look from shoulder to shoulder as if you are saying "no way." This allows the appropriate neck muscles to turn the head rather than to engage in voice production.

■ Maintain a consistent rate of head turning without moving other areas of the body.

■ The head turn may begin to slow or come to a stop when vocal tension increases—attention should be brought to this and addressed.

■ Cues can be given to alter the rate of the head turn (typically cues are given to increase the rate to help minimize vocal tension) based on the patient's response.

■ Visual feedback with a mirror can aid in monitoring the rate of the head turn.

II. Forward Bend (Figures 2–1A and 2–1B)

1. In a seated or standing position, whichever is more comfortable, bend over at the waist. Allow the head and arms to hang.

   a. Take note of areas of tension—the occipital region, shoulders, upper back, and so forth.

   b. Ask the patient to observe possible areas of tension and cue to release.

   c. Tactile feedback can be provided to aid in awareness and release (e.g., place the fingers and thumb at the base of the skull to increase awareness of tension in the occipital region and neck).

2. Begin to feel the breath observing habitual breathing patterns.

   a. Resume focus on the occipital region and cue for release during inhalation.

Figure 2–1A. Forward bend—seated. Photograph courtesy of Sarah Schneider.

Figure 2–1B. Forward bend—standing. Photograph courtesy of Sarah Schneider.

b. A head turn or nodding "yes" can be helpful in releasing the neck.

c. Focus on areas of expansion and deflation— rib cage, abdomen, and upper or lower back.

d. Bring attention to the areas that you would like to increase awareness and freedom. Provide tactile feedback for the patient as needed.

For example, place your hands on the lower rib cage/back and cue for expansion into your hands. Bring attention to that feeling. Focus on the expansion of the belly against the quadriceps (especially in a seated forward bend).

3. Begin vocalization.

a. Maintain release in targeted areas.

b. Continue to focus on practiced breathing patterns coordinated with voice production.

It is often easier to feel forward resonance in a forward bend.

4. Maintain target voice into the upright position.

a. Once the desired voice production is established, return to an upright position working to maintain ease and quality.

b. To aid in carryover and consistency, choose a specific focus when returning to the upright position.

i. The ease of voicing
ii. Fluid breathing
iii. The sensation of resonance

III. Lunge (Figure 2–2)

1. Begin vocalization. During an area of specific tension (e.g., reaching a "high" note), begin to employ the lunge by taking a large step forward with one foot. Bend into the knee while keeping the upper body in a neutral posture (do not let the knee pass over the foot during the knee bend).

2. Step back to midline.

3. Step forward with the other foot and bend into the knee. This is completed in succession as needed (and often results in burning in the quadriceps).

Note. Bending should take place on the "high" note or during the area of most difficulty.

Figure 2–2. Lunge. Photograph courtesy of Todd Schneider.

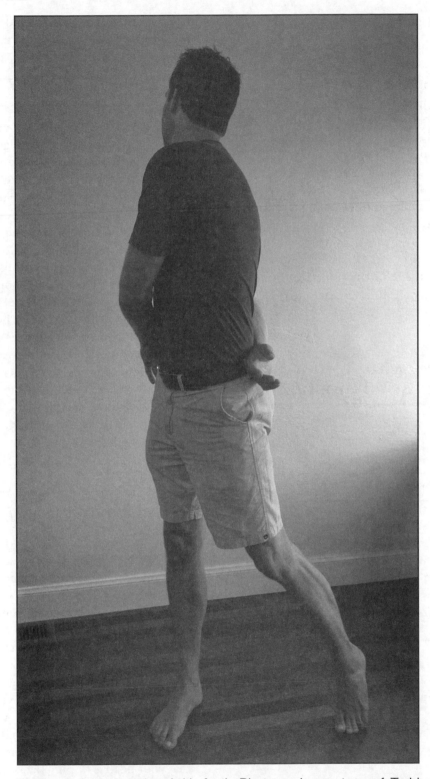

Figure 2–3. Arm swing (with foot). Photograph courtesy of Todd Schneider.

IV. Arm Swing (Figure 2–3)

1. Begin swinging the arms from side to side while turning the upper body. The arms are relaxed and swing into the body during each turn. The head turns with the upper body.
   a. The arms and shoulders should begin to release, and the rib cage should begin to loosen.
   b. Breathing should fall into a rhythm with the arm swing or vice versa.
   c. The upper body turn may be extended to the lower body, beginning to turn the opposite leg and foot (be careful not to turn at the knee).
2. Pair this with vocalization. Observe how the vocalization begins to move in rhythm with the breathing and arm swings. If not, the voice may begin to tighten and should be addressed.

Semi-Supine with Spinal Jiggle and Pelvic Bowl Slosh/Slide

Marya Spring Cordes

Purpose of Exercises

- To encourage alignment of the head, neck, back
- To engage ease and fluidity of subtle movement throughout the body
- To prepare the instrument for activity

Origin of Exercises

Based on theories of the Alexander Technique™, traditional acting, training, and Pilates, these exercises are intended to be executed prior to vocalization. It is a way of readying the instrument (the body) for working (singing/acting) with efficiency and economy by

> Vocalization is not meant to be conversational or melodic, but in rhythm with the breathing.

starting from a released state and adding movement/ effort into the equation in a layered way.

Overview of Exercises

This three-part readying warm-up begins with releasing excess tension with the gentle support from the floor or mat in a semi-supine position, giving the performer an easy sense of her/his head, neck, back relationship. The second part (Spinal Jiggle) of the readying warm-up encourages body awareness of how gentle movement travels from the toes to the head as one connected organism. The third part (Pelvic Slosh and Slide) allows for more vigorous movement, engaging larger muscle groups to encourage awareness of the musculature surrounding the spine that connect throughout the neck and back. The three parts, done in sequence, give the performer an opportunity to connect breath with released movement while lengthening the spine and freeing the neck. The readying can take as little as 5 minutes, but Part I could expand to any amount of time (maximum 20 minutes) that the individual has in her/his schedule.

Exercises

Part I: Releasing Excess Tension in a Semi-Supine Position

1. Lay on the floor or mat in a semi-supine position. Semi-supine means to be prone on your back with bent knees, so that the bottoms of your feet are maintaining gentle contact with the ground, and your knees are in an upward diagonal toward the ceiling. The palms of your hands should rest easily on your lower rib cage with your bent elbows resting on the floor or mat, forming a triangle with your hands and shoulders. Allow the elbows to ease out and away from the body as wide as comfortably possible without having to hold them there with a good deal of effort in your muscles. (If you sense that your head is tipping backward so that the back of your neck is shortening in this position, place a book under your head thick enough to provide a gentle lengthening of the muscles in the back of the neck, but not so thick as to make the chin tuck

toward the chest creating tension in the front of the neck.)

2. Give yourself as much time as you have in your schedule to be in this position because you have now employed gravity as your personal spine lengthener. While you are in semi-supine, keep your eyes open, and notice your breathing. Do not do anything to change it, just notice the gentle expansion and contraction of all of the musculature responding to the inhalation and exhalation of the respiratory process. Notice if you are holding yourself up off the floor/mat in any way and see if you can sink into the floor a bit more, spreading over it like butter spreading over a warm muffin. Keep your eyes open as you are noticing your breathing and allow your body to become a bit longer and a bit wider.

3. Easily allow your eyes only to look to the right, and with the least amount of effort, allow your head to gently roll to the right to meet them. Notice how easy and free this movement can be. Look easily with your eyes to center, and then see if you can, with even less effort than before, roll the head back to center. Repeat this process to the left and then back to center. Notice your breathing.

Part II: Spinal Jiggle

1. On an exhale, from your semi-supine position, allow one foot to slide out into a full supine position in the easiest way possible for you. Do not rush; it does not matter how long or how many inhales/exhales it takes you to do this. On an exhale, allow your other leg to slide into a full supine position. You now are lying completely on your back (in full supine) on the floor/mat with your arms, shoulders, and hands in a triangular relationship.

2. Allow yourself to anchor your heels easily to the ground and on your exhale, and point and flex your foot fully from the ankle joint in a relatively vigorous fashion. Allow the reciprocal movement to travel all the way up the body, traveling up through the connecting musculature of the legs and continuing up the spine, through the connector of the neck and up to the head. Rest on your inhale. Do this exertion on the exhale, resting on the inhale for three cycles. If you are allowing ease and noticing reciprocal motion, at the top of the body you will sense a gentle nodding "yes" with the head as it is poised easily on the top of the spine at the occipital joint. If you are not noticing a head nod without doing an intentional nodding of your head, check in with the ease of your neck by repeating Step 3 of Part I (looking with your eyes and rolling your head to where you are looking) in the inhale rest. Once three or four repetitions of the Spinal Jiggle are complete on exhales, rest on your inhale.

3. On your next exhale, utilize your core musculature to engage your abdomen muscles and allow them to bring your lower back in contact with the floor. Allow your knee to slowly bend to bring one foot sole in contact with the floor—back to a semi-supine position. Rest on your inhale. On your next exhale, engage your core musculature to bring your lower back in stronger contact with the floor. Allow the other knee to bend to bring the other leg to a semi-supine position. Return to noticing your breathing and release any residual work that remains in your muscles from the Spinal Jiggle into the floor.

Part III: Pelvic Bowl Slosh/Slide

1. On an exhale, allow the ground to easily come up through the legs as the feet push gently into the ground, engaging your hamstrings, quadriceps, and gluteus maximus and minimus, bringing the pelvis into a medium pelvic bridge (your hips and pelvic bowl will be elevated from the floor).

2. Inhale. On your next exhale, ask all of the excess work to release from your hamstrings, quadriceps, and gluteus maximus and minimus. This will lower the position of the pelvis in space a bit and will create a suspension of the pelvic structure above the ground, but with the least muscular effort as possible for the task.

3. As you are suspended, on an exhale, begin rotating your pelvic bowl around your spine. It will kinasense that the hips and pelvis are rotating right and left around the spine and sloshing water out of a bowl at the highest point in the rotation. Do this slowly and easily during your exhales and inhales for three or four breaths. Rest in the suspension and

make sure you are again releasing any extra work out of "holding the bridge." Rest two full breaths.

4. On an exhale again, begin moving the pelvis, this time in a lateral (nonrotating) movement. Slowly and easily, begin a slide of the pelvic bowl that is parallel to the ground right and left like Grandma's porch slider's movement. There should be no elevating and sloshing, only lateral right and left movement parallel to the ground, pushing the boundaries of right and left. Do this slowly and easily during your exhales and inhales for three or four breaths. Rest in the suspension and make sure you are again releasing any extra work out of "holding my bridge." Rest two full breaths.

5. On your next exhale, come down to the floor from your pelvic bridge rolling down your spine extremely slowly from the top vertebrae to your sacrum in a sequential fashion. Once you are in a full semi-supine, release all of the extra work from your musculature into the floor/mat and become aware again of the gentle in and out of the natural breath. If you kinasense tension in the front or back of the neck from the work of the slosh/slide, repeat Step 3 of Part I (looking with your eyes and rolling your head to where you are looking).

6. Find a way off the floor easily to standing, leaving the neck as easy as possible as you find your way into standing. You are now ready for a more athletic event. Take a walk, speak, and notice how the body/voice is different than before you went though the readying sequence.

Freeing the Neck and Shoulders

Marina Gilman

Purpose of Exercise

Tension in the neck and shoulders is common and often a source for increased laryngeal muscle tension. Neck and shoulder rolls are frequently trained during therapy to relieve the tension. However, they generally provide only temporary relief, and don't address the underlying discoordination of the neck and shoulder muscles. The habituated pattern remains. This exercise

(movement exploration) begins the process of reeducation of the nervous system.

This exploration is done in sitting. The purpose is to:

■ Facilitate reduction of extraneous neck and shoulder tension.
■ Free the upper trunk and optimize respiratory phonatory coordination (breathing and sound).

Origin of Exercise

This exercise (movement exploration) is based on the principles of the Feldenkrais Method®. The Feldenkrais method uses constraints to allow the nervous system to discover new movement options and promote increased awareness of the quality of these movements.

Overview of Exercise

This exploration is done sitting comfortably upright in a chair. Both feet on the floor.

The lesson consists of slow movements of each shoulder and the head, first individually and then in coordinated easy movement.

Exercise (Movement Exploration)

1. Sit comfortably upright in a chair. Place both feet on the floor.
   a. Notice how you are sitting.
   b. Think about your right shoulder and its relationship to your right ear. How do you sense the distance of your shoulder to your ear? Is the shoulder slightly forward or back of your ear? Compare that with the relationship of your left shoulder to your left ear. Is it the same for each side or are there slight differences? Just notice.
   c. Do you sense more tension on the one side than the other?
2. Slowly and gently begin to lift and lower your right shoulder towards your right ear. It is not important for them to touch. Just go in the general direction. Do this slowly at least 10 times.

a. Make sure your shoulder fully relaxes down each time.

b. Be sure to move slowly. Let the movement be as smooth as possible. For many at the beginning, movement may be jerky or uneven.

c. Notice the direction of the movement. Does it go straight up or at angle? Smooth or jagged?

d. Do not change the movement—just become aware what you are doing. Stay within the limits of ease and comfort. Allow the movement to gradually expand.

e. How is your breathing? Try to breathe in an easy regular pattern as you continue lifting and lowering your shoulder.

Stop and rest. Make sure your shoulders are relaxed.
Notice whether you are aware of any differences in the feeling of your right shoulder compared with your left. Has the quality of your breathing changed at all?

3. Gently begin to tilt your head towards your right shoulder. Think that you are bringing your right ear TOWARDS BUT NOT TO your right shoulder and back to a neutral upright position. Repeat this movement several times slowly.

a. Go slowly. What is the quality of this movement?

b. Think about your nose staying in the same plane, as though you had it gently pressed to a window and were trying to tilt your head to look out at something.

c. How are you breathing? Is it jerky, gentle, and even?

d. How much of your upper body is moving? Are you shifting your weight from side to side as you tilt your head towards your shoulder or letting your rib cage fold and expand?

e. Remember this is only about noticing. There is no right or wrong way of doing these movements.

Stop and rest.
Observe any changes you notice between the right and left side, in your breathing, in the way you are sitting.

4. Now combine these movements. Lift and lower your right shoulder and at the same time bring your right ear towards your shoulder, tilting your head. You are bringing your shoulder towards your ear and your ear TOWARDS (not to) your shoulder. Repeat several times slowly.

a. Go slowly; attend to your breathing.

b. What is the quality of the movement? Allow it to be free and not rushed.

Stop and rest.
Observe any differences between your right side and your left side. Allow your attention to go to your breathing, the way you are sitting, your face. Notice any differences between your right and left side.

5. Gently and slowly begin to lift and lower your LEFT shoulder towards your LEFT ear. Do this movement many times slowly. Does it feel different than on the left side? Repeat several times slowly.

a. As with the right side, pay attention to the quality of the movement of your shoulder. How are you breathing?

Stop and rest.

6. Gently begin to tilt your head towards your left shoulder, bringing your left ear TOWARDS BUT NOT TO your left shoulder. Be sure to let your shoulder release all the way. Repeat several times slowly.
Keep the movement simple and light. Do not strain or force yourself to go farther than is easy.

Stop and rest.
Observe any changes you notice between the left and right side in your breathing, in the way you are sitting.

7. Begin to lift and lower your left shoulder and at the same time bring your left ear towards your shoulder, tilting your head. You are bringing your left shoulder towards your left ear and your left ear TOWARDS (not to) your left shoulder. Repeat several times slowly.
Keep the movement light and easy. Be sure each time to fully release your shoulder as you bring your head fully upright.

REST
Compare your right side and your left side. Stand and observe any changes you notice in the way you are sitting. Stand. Notice the way in which you feel your feet contact the floor. **Try to vocalize a little. Is there any change in the ease or quality of your voice?**

Balancing Your Head

Marina Gilman

Purpose of Exercise

What constitutes "correct" singing posture is totally dependent on the style of singing and the demands of performance. Postural challenges can arise when singing with the stationary microphone, either standing or suspended, as commonly found in a recording studio. The challenge is how to lean into the mic in such a way as to maintain optimal airflow and comfort in the neck and upper torso. This exercise is designed to:

- Help the singer find the most dynamically efficient posture for the head and chest.
- Help the singer find the internal organization that allows for the best and most communicative vocal expression.

Origin of Exercise

This exercise (movement exploration) is based on the principles of the Feldenkrais Method®. The Feldenkrais method uses constraints to allow the nervous system to discover new movement options and promote increased awareness of the quality of these movements.

Overview of Exercise

In this movement exploration the body is placed in a position of optimal stability. In standing, the trunk is bent at the hip joints—not at the waist—the hands are on the thighs, elbows slightly bent, and the fingers pointing towards one another. In this position the back is straight, allowing freedom of movement in the spine and abdominal muscles. It is very important that the back is straight and long with the eyes looking down and slightly forward, allowing the neck to be an extension of the straight spine.

The exploration is of the head—forward, back, gradually allowing the whole spine to move with the head and neck. The exploration begins without

voicing, but voice is added to reinforce the awareness of optimal movement.

All movements are to be done **slowly** and with attention to the quality of the movement. Range is not important. Always stay within your comfort level. *Remember there is no right or wrong way to do these movements so long as they are not strained.*

Exercise (Movement Exploration)

Position: Stand with feet comfortably apart, leaning slightly forward with the back straight, elbows gently bent and fingers facing one another. Imagine you have a tail and lift it slightly so the pelvis does not round under. The head is in line with the spine. The gazing point is slightly forward and down. Shoulders are relaxed.

1. In this position slowly move your head forward and back. Repeat 10 to 20 times slowly. Begin.
   a. Notice how your neck is moving.
   b. Is the movement just from the head? Does it involve the jaw or chest?
   c. What is happening with your breathing? Can it stay easy or does it stop at certain points?
2. Stop and rest. Stand up. Take a few steps around yourself. Has anything changed?
3. Resume the same position. This time initiate the movement of the head forward and back from your chin, bringing it forward and back. Keep repeating this movement 10 to 20 times slowly.
   a. Does this feel different than when you just moved your head forward and then back?
   b. What is happening in your chest or back? Do you sense any movement?
   c. Notice how this subtle shift in attention to where the movement is initiated changes the flow.
   d. Some of you might not feel any change, if this is your habitual way of moving.
   e. Sense if the movement is just in the neck. Or is there slight movement in the sternum as well?
   f. What is happening with your breathing? Can it stay easy or does it stop at certain points?

Stop and rest. Stand up and take a few steps around.
4. Resume the same position. This time initiate the movement of the head forward and back from your

forehead. Keep repeating this movement 10 times slowly.

  a. What is the trajectory of your head? Does your chin want to move at some point?

  b. What is happening in your chest or back? Do you sense any movement?

  c. Does this feel different than when you just moved your head forward and then back?

  d. Notice how this subtle shift in attention to where the movement is initiated changes the flow. Some of you might not feel any change, if this is your habitual way of moving.

  e. What is happening with your breathing? Can it stay easy or does it stop at certain points?

Stop and rest. Stand up and take a few steps around. Notice any change in how you stand/your breath/feeling in your neck.

5. Still standing comfortably, begin to vocalize lightly on a lip trill (raspberry), tongue trill (rolled *r*), or some buzzy sound. Notice how it feels.

6. Resume the same position. Once again initiate the movement of the head forward and back as you did at the beginning, only this time as you move your head forward and back, vocalize on the buzzy sound. Keep repeating this movement 10 times slowly.

  a. What happens to the flow of the sound? Is it easy to keep the sound going or does it want to stop or does it become more difficult?

Stop and rest for a moment.

7. In the same position, vocalize while moving your head forward and back, initiating the movement from your chin.

  a. Does this change the ease of quality of the sound? Does the flow and/or color of your sound change in quality or ease as your head moves forward and back?

  b. Is the movement just in the neck and head, or is your spine becoming more involved?

Stop and rest for a moment.

8. In the same position, vocalize while moving your head forward and back, initiating the movement from your forehead.

  a. Does this change the ease of quality of the sound?

Stop and rest for a moment.

9. Stand comfortably and just vocalize in the same way you have been. Pretend there is a stationary microphone in front of you. Adjust yourself towards the mic and notice if there is any change from your normal habitual sensations.

Climbing the Ladder

Caroline Helton

Purpose of Exercise

■ To stretch and elongate the torso
■ To energize the entire body
■ To activate the muscles of the thorax to expand the rib cage

Origin of Exercise

After having the pleasure and privilege of being instructed in movement and body warm-ups by Prof. Annette Masson (my colleague in the Drama department at the UM School of Music, Theatre and Dance), I have adapted one of her many helpful exercises aimed at loosening and energizing the body. Students who use these kinds of stretches before they practice or perform uniformly report much greater freedom and comfort in their bodies and ease of vocal production.

Exercise

1. Stand with the feet shoulder-width apart and reach up first with one arm and then with the other, as if you were climbing a ladder. It's important to really actively mime ladder climbing, or else the thoracic muscles won't fully engage.

2. Take special care to keep the neck and shoulders relaxed and to look up while you "climb the ladder," so that you don't overcompensate in muscle groups that we don't need to engage when we sing.

3. Do this continuously for 20 to 30 seconds and then bend over at the waist and shake out the shoulders and arms.

4. Repeat these two steps as many times as necessary to feel energized, stretched, and fully engaged in the thorax.

Anterior Chest Openers to Improve Posture

Jill Vonderhaar Nader

Purpose of Exercises

To open the chest wall to increase range of motion of the upper body for contemporary commercial music (CCM) singing.

Origin of Exercises

The exercises below stem from traditional physical therapy exercises. These are useful for CCM singers, who are often also dancers with reduced range of motion of the rib cage and abdomen because of extensive dance training resulting in tight ribs and abdomen.

Exercises

1. Lower Trapezius "V" Exercise
   Stand facing a wall with arms overhead in a "V" shape. Point your thumbs out ("hitchhiker position"). Inhale deeply and slide your shoulder blades up toward your ears to stretch. Then exhale deeply and slide your shoulder blades down and in toward your spine. Think about making the bottom of the capital V shape. Do not just slide straight down—focus on sliding the tips of your scapulae down and in one motion. Keep the front of your ribs pulled in—don't arch your back (Figure 2–4). Hold 3 seconds. Repeat 10 times.
2. Pectoralis Release
   Using a small ball such as a lacrosse ball or a Franklin ball, stand facing a wall. Place one arm straight out to your side at shoulder level with the palm of your hand flat to the wall. Move your head away from your arm. Place the ball directly above the nipple line against your chest. Lean in slightly toward the ball and move your body side to side, rolling the ball toward your front shoulder. Try to stay directly on the chest and don't force the ball into the front of your shoulder. If you feel a tight spot, hold it and breathe deeply for five breaths (Figure 2–5).
3. Foam Roller Upper Back Release
   Using a half or full foam roller (can be purchased at optp.com), sit on the floor with the roller placed horizontally across your lower back. Your knees are bent and feet flat on the floor. Place your hands behind your head to support your neck. Slowly start to roll the roller up your back using your legs to help you push the roller. Start easy and just roll from your tailbone up to the space between the shoulder blades a few times. As you feel more comfortable, start to arch your upper back over the roller then roll back up. Try to exhale as you arch over the roller and allow your chest to open. Roll through the back and midback for about 2 minutes (Figure 2–6).
4. Side of the Chest/Rib Cage Opener
   Opening the lateral chest is very important to allow for maximum lung capacity as well as to improve mobility in your back and chest.
   Lie on the foam roller on your side with your bottom arm outstretched and the roller under your ribs a few inches below the armpit. The top arm can reach overhead to stretch. Your knees can be bent up and rest on the floor. Try to hold this position and take some slow deep breaths into the tight areas. Start with 15 seconds and build up to 1 minute or longer. You can also move it around to try different areas of the lateral rib cage. Switch sides (Figure 2–7).

Lower Back Expansion

Sarah Maines

Purpose of Exercise

■ To release tension in the lower back and promote efficient alignment

Figure 2–4. Lower trapezius "V" exercise. Photograph courtesy of Wendy LeBorgne.

■ To encourage a deeper, three-dimensional expansion for inhalation

of body alignment and tension release found in the Alexander Technique™, the Feldenkrais Method®, and Pilates.

Origin of Exercise

Many CCM singers must perform or rehearse while seated, and complain of back/shoulder tension and/or decreased breath capacity. Often, these singers are exaggerating the arch in their lumbar spine in order to "sit up straight." This exercise is inspired by principles

Overview of Exercise

A large stability ball and a chair are needed for this exercise. The exercise may be used for singers who suffer from decreased breath capacity and tension from misalignment through the lumbar spine. Singers will

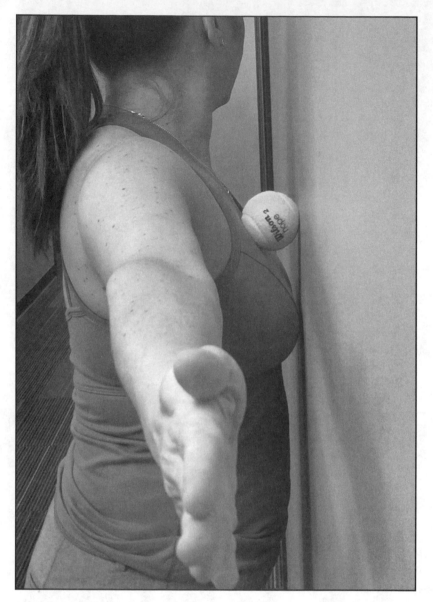

Figure 2–5. Pectoralis release. Photograph courtesy of Wendy LeBorgne.

assess their current norm, use the stability ball and then the chair to experience a lengthened lumbar spine, and then return to the first step to compare the difference in alignment and breath expansion. Pitches should remain in optimum comfort range for each individual singer. Although any vowel/consonant combination may be used, semi-occluded sounds (lip trill, tongue trill, raspberry, etc.) that maintain optimum air flow through phonation are initially encouraged.

Exercise

Step 1

Sit in a chair with normal singing posture and sing a moderately slow, forte five-note scale on your favorite semi-occluded sound (lip trill, tongue trill, raspberry, etc.). Repeat, moving up and down by semitones in the most comfortable part of your range. Draw your

Figure 2–6. Foam roller upper back release. Photograph courtesy of Wendy LeBorgne.

Figure 2–7. Side of the chest/rib cage opener. Photograph courtesy of Wendy LeBorgne.

attention to the expansion of your lower back as you inhale. You do not have to change anything: simply notice how your lower back feels upon inhalation. If you typically hold a score or other music during rehearsal, find a score to hold and repeat the exercise, paying special attention to how your lower back feels (Figure 2-8).

Step 2

Kneel in front of the stability ball, and then lie forward on the ball to "give it a hug" with your abdomen and chest resting on the ball. Turn your chin to one side and allow your head and arms to release, so they simply hang around the ball. Breathe deeply, noticing

the expansion of your abdominals into the ball upon inhalation. Next, notice the simultaneous expansion of your lower back. Spend as long as you like in this position, exploring this feeling of length and width through the lumbar spine. Now, sing the same five-note scale pattern from Step 1 as best you can while lying on the ball. Notice the difference in the lower back upon inhalation (Figure 2-9).

Step 3

Sit in a chair with your feet shoulder-width apart and your heels directly beneath your knees. Lean forward to rest your elbows on your knees. Repeat the deep breathing and five-note scale pattern, maintaining as

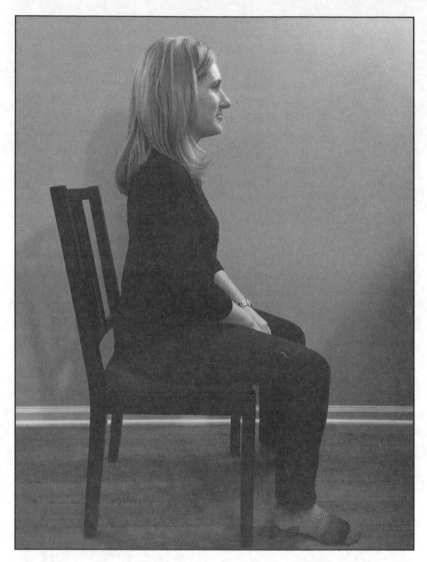

Figure 2–8. Normal sitting posture.

much sensation of length and width in the lower back as possible (Figure 2–10).

Step 4

Sit upright in a chair and repeat the deep breathing and five-note scale pattern, maintaining as much sensation of length and width in the lower back as possible. Use negative practice to further explore this new alignment: overarch your lumbar spine and repeat the deep breathing and five-note scale pattern, then release the lower back to lengthen and widen the lower back upon inhalation (Figure 2–11). Imagine the ischium, or "sit bones" lengthening through the chair toward the floor as you inhale. Again, if you typically hold a score or other music during rehearsal, find a folder to hold and repeat the exercise, paying special attention to maintaining your new lumbar spine alignment and three-dimensional breath (Figure 2–12).

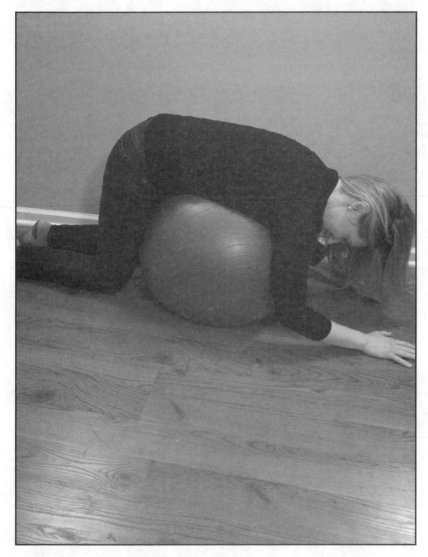

Figure 2–9. Kneeling on stability ball.

Figure 2–10. Leaning forward.

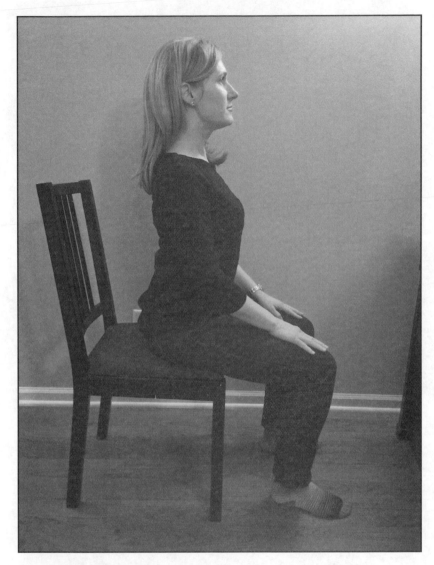

Figure 2–11. Overarching back.

Figure 2–12. Balanced alignment holding score.

Postural Alignment, Core Strength, and Breath Support

Suzan Postel

Purpose of Exercise

■ To facilitate neutral postural alignment
■ To activate the core muscles
■ To stabilize the shoulder girdle and pelvic girdle

■ To facilitate lateral and back rib expansion and breath support

Origin of Exercise

This exercise is based on the principles of Pilates, Alexander technique, and somatic awareness. I use it to correct the posture pattern I commonly observe in singers: forward head and shoulders, rib cage pulled up, tight low back and psoas.

Overview of Exercise

This exercise integrates postural alignment and optimized breathing to build strength and freedom in singers' whole body instrument. It is done face down in a prone position to facilitate lateral and back rib breathing and to strengthen the back of the body for postural support. We activate the core muscles to support the pelvis and lumbar spine and we engage the scapular stabilizers to support the shoulder girdle and thoracic spine while using the least amount of muscle tension necessary to create a balance between freedom and stability. We end by standing and observing any postural changes that have occurred, then add vocalization to integrate these changes into the whole body vocal instrument.

Exercise

Breathing and Core Activation

Position: Lie face down on a mat or firmly padded surface with legs extended, sitz bones width apart, and tops of feet on the ground. Rest your forehead on the backs of your hands with elbows wide, palms down, and fingers interlaced (Figure 2–13) below the palms so that the fingers are on the ground, creating a hollow for your forehead. (If this is uncomfortable, place one hand on top of the other.)

1. Allow the weight of the skeleton to release into the mat, and notice how the lower (lumbar) curve of your back is slightly exaggerated due to the body's relation to gravity in prone position (Figure 2–14). Inhale as though you could breathe all the way down to your sitz bones, and observe the space between the rib cage and pelvis expanding into length and width, restoring your natural (neutral) lumbar curve (Figure 2–15).

2. Keeping the bottom front ribs and pubic bone in contact with the mat, exhale while drawing the abdominal area up towards the lumbar spine, so the abdominals are supporting your low back in its expanded (neutral) curve (Figure 2–16). Release the belly on the inhale. Repeat.

   a. Did you feel your abdominal muscles engage?

   b. Could you isolate the abdominals without engaging the gluteal (butt) and shoulder muscles?

Figure 2–13. Hand position. Photo courtesy of Suzan Postel.

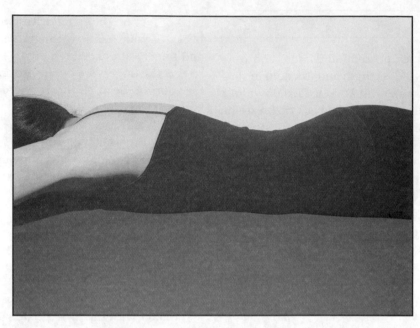

Figure 2–14. Increased lumbar curve. Photo courtesy of Suzan Postel.

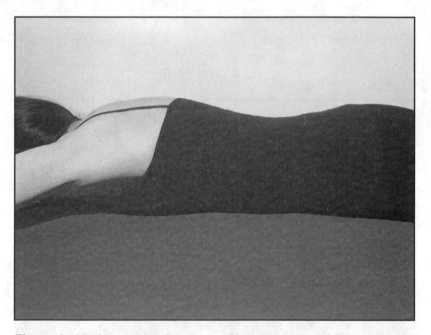

Figure 2–15. Neutral lumbar curve. Photo courtesy of Suzan Postel.

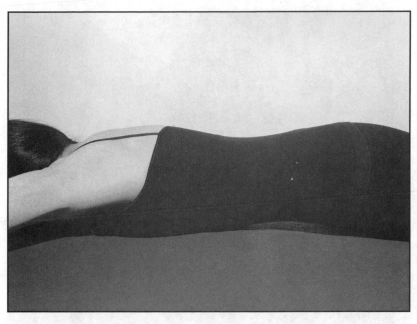

Figure 2–16. Abdominals supporting the lumbar spine. Photo courtesy of Suzan Postel.

3. Keep the abdominals engaged on both the inhale and the exhale. Repeat two or three times.
   a. Do you feel the abdominal work intensify when staying engaged on the inhale?
   b. Do you feel the back and side ribs expand more when holding the belly in on inhalation?
   Although during singing inhalation we want to release the belly to allow full downward excursion of the diaphragm, we can use Step 3 as a practice tool to strengthen the abdominals (exhalation muscles) by keeping them engaged on the inhale, and to train the external intercostals (inhalation muscles) to keep the rib cage expanded on exhalation.

4. **Shoulder girdle stabilization.** Inhale with shoulders released (Figure 2–17). Exhale, sinking your upper chest towards the mat while widening the elbows and collar bones apart so they create a gentle pull on your interlaced fingers. Without moving the forearms, gently press into the thumb sides of the forearms as though you were sliding them towards the top of the mat, and allow this action to slide the shoulders down towards your pelvis in opposition (Figure 2–18).
   a. Do you feel activation around the sides and bottom of your shoulder blades (scapulae)?

   b. Are your shoulder blades lying flatter across your back ribs?
5. Sit back towards your heels (only as far as is comfortable for your back and knees) to release your back in child's pose. Then, without lifting your head, slowly rise to standing with as little effort as possible, and wait for your head to float on top of your spine like a helium balloon. Close your eyes and observe any new sensations, without judging or trying to fix anything.

Do you feel more grounded through your feet?

Do you feel energy rising through the center of your trunk, neck, and head?

Does your pelvis feel heavier and more released?

Do your back ribs feel propped up and open? Do your lower front ribs feel released and hanging from the spine?

Do you feel more movement of the breath in the trunk and pelvis without actively making it happen?

Do you feel a subtle sense of activation in the abdominal area?

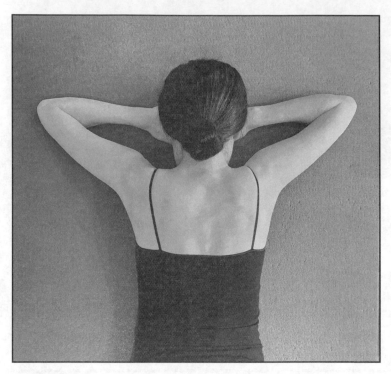

Figure 2–17. Shoulders released. Photo courtesy of Suzan Postel.

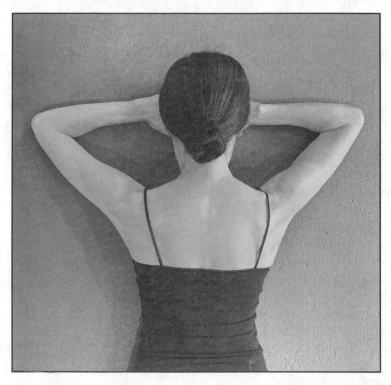

Figure 2–18. Shoulders stabilized. Photo courtesy of Suzan Postel.

Add gentle vocalization such as hums, sirens, or lip trills while maintaining awareness of these new sensations. When old patterns or tensions creep back in, just notice, pause to release them, and begin again. Over time you will be increasingly able to sustain this awareness, and your default patterns will gradually shift towards healthier function.

Reorganizing the Entire Vocal Tract

Robert C. Sussuma

Purpose of Exercise

The purpose of the following experience is to bring more awareness, mobility, coordination, and integration to the vocal tract. When done slowly, precisely, and with sensitive attention, this lesson has the power to reset how we hold and use the mouth, head, neck, and throat. It can be used as a general learning tool as well as preparation for any vocal task. The movement sequences, once well-known and integrated, can also be tailored for specific vocal learning goals and intentions. No matter what your aim, this lesson will bring balance and proportionality to your vocal tract while increasing your vocal awareness, setting the scene for easy, functional speaking and singing.

Origin of Exercise

This is an original Awareness Through Movement® (ATM) lesson created by Robert Sussuma, Guild-Certified Feldenkrais Practitioner (GCFP). Though inspired by basic functional movements of the vocal tract, this lesson transforms those movements into a Feldenkrais®-style lesson that utilizes the principles of the Feldenkrais Method of Somatic Education to bring about improved vocal action through experiential learning and reorganization. This lesson is the culmination of years of personal practice and teaching, an intimate knowledge of vocal anatomy and function, as well as a practical understanding of sensorimotor

learning principles. It has the potential to not only bring about positive physical changes, but can also update the learner's nervous system through clarifying the self-image of the vocal tract for improved vocal ability.

Overview of Exercise

Technically, this is not an exercise, but rather a "lesson" because unlike an exercise, there is no particular technical aim or goal associated with the experience. Although what you will explore is related to specific physical coordination, the true aim is learning. What that will mean for each person will be different and will depend on her/his current ability, awareness, and physical organization. Instead of thinking of it as an exercise, think of it as a systematic exploration of various functional vocal possibilities with awareness. This open-ended approach allows for it to be both a universal and a personal experience. As the style of instruction invites learners to adapt and adjust based on their own experience along the way, it can be useful for students of any level and ability. If you are new to this kind of learning, remember: As long as you stay curious and avoid discomfort, there is no wrong way to do this.

Exercise

Due to the experiential nature of this kind of learning, this lesson has been recorded and is available in the audio materials section that accompanies this edition of *The Vocal Athlete*. It is impossible to understand what this lesson is really about and what it has to offer without actually doing it, so take the time to listen to the recording and follow the instructions given.

The first section of the lesson includes a scan that invites an awareness of sensations in preparation for the movements and learning to come. In a classic scan, one senses certain parts of the body before movement is introduced. This also serves to enhance proprioception and accuracy throughout the process. You will also be asked to speak or sing something as a reference before the lesson begins. This allows you to track any changes that may have come about in your singing as a result of the process.

The second section of the lesson focuses on various movements intended to reorganize the entirety of the tongue, from tip to base. Starting in this section, and continuing throughout the lesson, the forefingers of each hand (see Figure 2–19) are extended and placed in the following positions: the tip of the forefinger of one hand touching the tip of the tongue as it "floats" in the center of the mouth and the tip of the forefinger of the other hand placed on the neck, directly in front of the center of the hyoid bone (see

Figures 2–20 and 2–21 for a front and side view of the positions).

This section employs a movement constraint for learning. The constraint is that the hyoid bone (and the forefinger touching it) do not move at all while the tongue (and the forefinger touching it) move in various ways.

In the third section of the lesson, the focus is on the movement of the hyoid bone relative to the tongue. Conversely, the finger/hyoid connection moves

Figure 2–19. Fingers pointing.

Figure 2–20. Fingers touching tongue and hyoid, front view.

while the finger/tongue connection remains fixed in space.

In the fourth and final section, various configurations of the tongue and hyoid are explored while the fingers remain touching the tip of the tongue and the front of the hyoid, respectively. Various sounds are added to the movements as well as facial and emotional gestures. In the end, you will be asked to return to the same speaking or singing reference from the beginning and use it to notice any changes that have occurred in your vocalizing.

Conclusion

The vocal tract is made up of many structures that cooperate, working interdependently to create various complex movements, shapes, and configurations that,

Figure 2–21. Fingers touching tongue and hyoid, side view.

in combination with various breath and tone options, form the basis for most human vocal sounds and noises. All of this is orchestrated, of course, by our brain and nervous system through our intention and awareness. By working with <u>how</u> the vocal tract is organized, one can continuously improve one's ability to speak and sing. Learning to organize and reorganize the vocal tract in various ways, with various intentions, not only brings more ease and comfort for voicing in the ways one is already familiar with, but can also lead to new abilities, novel sounds, and expanded vocal color.

Once you have completed listening to and experiencing the recorded lesson in its entirety (perhaps several times), it is possible to take parts of the lesson and repeat the movements and sounds in your own way in order to recall the sensations and remind yourself of the particular organization that comes about in the entire vocal tract as a result of this unique experience.

Notes

3

Stretches and Exercises
for Breathing

Physical Stretching for Optimal Rib Cage and Respiratory Muscle Expansion

Erin N. Donahue and Wendy D. LeBorgne

Purpose of Exercise

- To gently stretch the muscles involved in respiration for thoracic and abdominal expansion during respiration
- To gain physical awareness of respiratory musculature prior to phonation
- To free any respiratory muscular restrictions through active stretching
- To center the breath

Origin of Exercise

This exercise is adapted from the physical therapy and exercise physiology literature to actively stretch muscles prior to activity. Because we have become a society that often sits at desks and in cars and spends much of our lives hunched over cell phones, the muscles of respiration often become compressed. Therefore, this sequence of exercises was designed as a means to actively expand and lengthen the muscles of respiration prior to singing tasks. Similar stretches may be performed prior to physical activity to aid in optimal thoracic muscle expansion prior to exercise.

Overview of Exercise

This gentle whole-body stretch targets thoracic and abdominal musculature during active inhalation and exhalation. Because vocal athletes are in constant motion, this exercise is designed to center the body and breath simultaneously. As with any stretch, the element of breathing through the stretch is vital. Therefore, maximal inhalation and exhalation cues are provided for the singer completing this exercise series. The exercise consists of lateral rib cage expansion, anterior posterior thoracic expansion, lateral stretching to increase the space between the superior hip (iliac crest), and the inferior rib cage bilaterally.

Exercise

1. Begin in an upright position. Clasp hands together in front of the body, keeping shoulders in a neutral position (do not round the shoulders forward; ensure your shoulders are not elevated). Then, inhale

slowly while stretching arms up over the head (keeping hands clasped together). Allow the elbows to bend only slightly, and keep arms extended. Turn palms outward to facilitate maximal stretch with optimal posture. Inhale completely and allow the rib cage to fully expand in all directions (lateral and front to back). Keep head neutral (balanced on the spine) with a relaxed neck (Figure 3–1).

2. Exhale slowly while stretching arms over to the left. Maintain thoracic expansion and arms outstretched. Hands should remain clasped. Maintain a neutral hip and pelvic position (i.e., ensure your hips are over your knees and that your chest is not in front of your hips). This stretch should be felt as a lateral stretch from the bottom of the right side of the rib cage to the top of the right side of the hip. Remain in this position for 5 to 10 seconds (Figure 3–2).

3. Release and stretch upward back to center while slowly inhaling (attempting to expand just a bit farther than the first stretch). Arms remain outstretched overhead with clasped hands. Continue to stretch upward with an elevated chest, neutral head position, and relaxed neck. Inhale completely and allow the rib cage to fully expand (see Figure 3–1).

4. Exhale slowly while stretching arms over to the right. Keep the chest elevated and arms outstretched straight. Hands should remain clasped. Maintain a neutral hip and pelvic position. A stretch should be felt from the bottom of the left side of the rib cage to the top of the right side of the hip. Remain in this position for 5 to 10 seconds (Figure 3–3).

5. Release back to center while slowly inhaling. Arms remain outstretched with clasped hands. Continue to stretch upward with an elevated chest, neutral

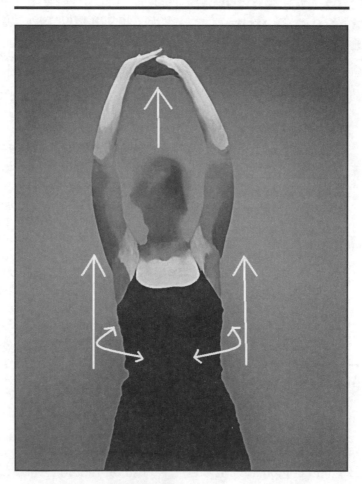

Figure 3–1. Upright position.

Figure 3–2. Stretching arms over to the left.

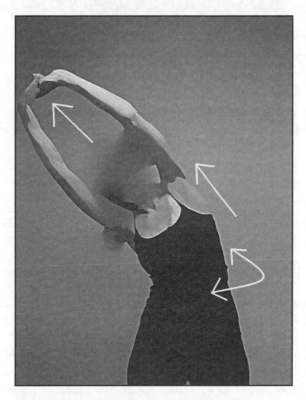

Figure 3–3. Stretching arms over to the right.

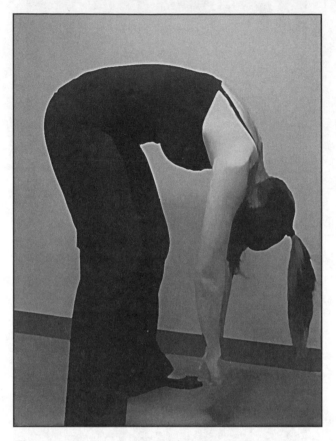

Figure 3–4. Bending body forward.

head position, and relaxed neck. Inhale completely and allow the rib cage to fully expand (see Figure 3–1).

6. Slowly begin to bring arms forward, over the head, and to the front of the body, while exhaling. Imagine that the top of your head is at the highest peak of a rollercoaster, and your spine is going to follow your head as you cascade downward on the exhale. Continue to exhale, and begin to bend the body forward. Keep knees relaxed and loose. Allow arms to release and hang toward the ground as the body is fully bent over. Ensure that the neck is loose. While in the slightly upside down position, wiggle your knees, then hips, then lower back, mid-back, and head during the course of several inhalations and exhalations. Note any areas of restriction or tension. Mentally focus on those areas and see if you can release those tensions (Figure 3–4).

7. Bend your knees and, gradually, begin to roll back up (stacking one vertebra on top of the next) while slowly inhaling, until an upright position is reached.

Ensure proper posture is maintained with relaxed shoulders and neck.

8. Repeat this sequence several times for maximal benefit.

Finding the Abs

Joan Melton

Purpose of Exercises

The following exercises are designed to help the hybrid singer—indeed, anyone involved in vocal performance—access efficient breath management strategies for a wide variety of performance situations. They focus on allowing the body to breathe in without effort and on matching the action of exhalation to the material, venue, and style.

Origin of Exercises

The first exercise uses a yoga-based Sphinx posture to help free the lower abdominals on inhalation and encourage their engagement (in and up) on exhalation, or while sounding. A similar exercise appears in One Voice: *Integrating Singing and Theatre Voice Techniques* (Melton/Tom, 2nd ed., Waveland, 2012, pp. 11-12). The second is based on a multitask item in the research protocol of a voice study done at the University of Queensland (Hodges/Melton, 2010). The twisted position while speaking or singing tends to wake up the abdominals, even for performers who are habitually "high breathers."

Overview of Exercises

Moving the action of breath management to the lower torso immediately connects *voice* to the whole person, so that we are no longer "disembodied" or a "talk-ing head." And allowing the body to breathe in on its own—rather than "taking" a breath—tends to eliminate audible inhalations, or gasps, that interrupt the story and call attention to themselves.

Exercises

Exercise 1

Stretch out on your belly (prone) on the floor, or on a mat or rug. Release any holding you may notice in the buttocks and legs; then bring yourself into the position of a Sphinx—forearms on the ground, shoulders down, back of the neck long and free, upper torso in an easy arch. Stretch the tongue out gently, open the eyes wide, and be sure to maintain width in the pharynx as you release gentle staccatos on indefinite pitches (Figure 3–5).

■ Use huh, huh, huh, huh (or hah, hah, hah, hah), then double time, triple time, and finally, one long huh, or hah. Be careful not to overdo the /h/. It should be barely there. Belly releases downward (toward the floor) between sounds—so only one

Figure 3–5. Modified Sphinx. Photograph courtesy of Christopher Chwee.

sound per breath; lower abs engage in and up (toward the spine) when you are sounding.

■ Alternatively, use an unvoiced fricative, as in the Accent Method (e.g., /sh/ in a variety of simple rhythms).

■ Or sing that song you were having trouble with and notice how easy the breathing becomes, and how you may suddenly *feel* differently about what you're saying.

Always follow the Sphinx or any other arch with a rounding of the body to protect the back. Leave your arms outstretched and sit back on your heels (as in yoga child's pose). Knees may be either together or separated. This is a wonderful position in which to siren through your whole pitch range, especially high to low (Figure 3–6). Move in any way you like and allow the voice to move as well.

Exercise 2

Sit cross-legged on the floor or on the edge of a straight chair or stool. Turn your upper torso fully to the right or left without moving the pelvis—so your lower torso and legs remain stable while your head and upper body face to the side (Figure 3–7). Shoulders are balanced and free. This will feel strange and is meant to be a bit challenging!

Again use staccatos on huh or hah, or speak bits of text, exploring all of your pitch range. Allow the *body* to match the action of the abs to whatever you are doing vocally, so that the amount of effort is never too much or too little.

■ Then sing a simple song—or anything else you like—noticing what happens in the abs as you do. Chances are they'll let go for effortless, silent inhalations and engage to "support" whatever sounds you make.

■ Now gently realign your upper body with the pelvis, so you are facing front; then do the exercise on the other side.

Finally, having felt that remote control, or release and engagement of low abdominals under your sound, begin to move as you sing—first on the floor, then gradually to standing. If you lose your "remote" at any

Figure 3–6. Crouch, or modified child's pose. Photograph courtesy of Christopher Chwee.

Figure 3–7. Twist. Photograph courtesy of Christopher Chwee.

point, go back to the floor! With daily practice, this basic strategy becomes your default and will get you through virtually any performance challenge.

Breath Management Strategy for Vocal Percussion

Bari Hoffman Ruddy and Adam Lloyd

Purpose of Exercise

- To reduce vocal hyperfunction during vocal percussive productions by managing respiratory drive
- To reduce vocal fatigue in vocal percussion performers

Origin of Exercise

Vocal percussion performers are a unique group of vocal athletes. They are usually small in number, if not the only ones in a group of performers producing the percussive sounds. Their performance requires loud and explosive sounds to be produced from the larynx and the supraglottic articulators. A substantial amount of subglottal or intraoral air pressure is required to produce the glottal stops, oral fricatives, or laryngeal fricatives that create the percussion-like sounds and other instrumental effects (Sapienza & Hoffman Ruddy, 2012). The concepts presented in this exercise are derived from a combination of breathing exercises utilized by sprint athletes as well as principles of laryngeal relaxation (Roy & Leeper, 1993), given the nature of rapid breath "reloading" that is required for the vocal percussion task.

Overview of Exercise

Vocal percussion performers need to be able to get air in quickly; therefore, this exercise promotes a strategy of breath management in order to maintain their busy and long percussive lines. Since some percussive sounds require more effort and varied pressure, this exercise provides a strategy of producing the sounds with the least amount of extrinsic effort as possible. It is important to help the performer find their threshold of effort, find times to relax the larynx, and monitor for excessive strain and tension. Increasing stamina is also imperative as syncope is a common occurrence among (untrained) vocal percussion performers. The concepts of this exercise can be carried over into any song or tempo that a vocal percussion artist performs.

Exercise

1. Begin by producing a slow rhythmic pant (i.e., two short inhalations followed by a forced exhalation). It may be helpful to lay on the floor initially and feel a complete relaxation of the abdomen and thorax. The abdomen should expand during the inhalation and gently contract during exhalation. Breathing in through the mouth and nose at the same time can be useful for getting more air in during a short duration of time. Slowly increase the speed of the pant until it is up to the desired tempo.

2. Next, repeat Step 1; this time begin to make sound during the exhalation (such as a short lip buzz or /bah/). A mirror can be used for visual feedback. Pay attention to keep the larynx in a relaxed, semilowered position. Relax the tongue and the jaw and find the threshold for effort in order to produce the intended sounds.

3. Next alternate a lip buzz and exhalation through the teeth "tss" (inhalation . . . lip buzz . . . inhalation . . . "tss" . . . inhalation . . . etc.). Easy percussive sounds should also be incorporated such as a crash cymbal or a base drum. To produce a crash cymbal, produce "chish" by clenching your teeth and not producing the vowel, going from "ch" straight to "sh" with little or no transition. The base drum requires you to produce the /b/ sound with your lips closed, letting the pressure build up before release.

> Prior to this exercise, performing stretching and massage techniques can help to promote laryngeal relaxation prior to initiating more intensive percussive sounds.

It is necessary to control the release of your lips just enough to let them vibrate for a short amount of time. To make the sound louder, you will need to produce lip oscillations by letting air vibrate through the lips similar to blowing a raspberry.

It is important for vocal percussionists to slowly practice breathing while producing each percussive sound independently (separating the breathing from the beat). Once this breathing technique is mastered (i.e., keeping up with the beat/tempo), another option is to also breathe in during several sounds that are produced on inhalation such as variations on the snare and handclap sounds. This allows several kinds of bass sounds, snare sounds, and even hi-hat sounds to continue without pausing to (re)breathe.

Breathing Body Release Visualization

Suzan Postel

Purpose of Exercise

I designed this to be done at the beginning of a lesson or practice session to:

- Increase somatic awareness
- Release physical and mental tension
- Optimize respiratory movement of the rib cage and abdomen
- Restore the parasympathetic nervous system
- Explore vocalization in this more balanced, released state

Origin of Exercise

This practice evolved from my personal explorations in preparing my mind and body for singing, and from observing how it applies to my individual students. It is based on the principles of Alexander technique, Mindfulness Meditation, Somatic Awareness, and my own imagery.

Overview of Exercise

The exercise is performed lying down in semi-supine position ("constructive rest") with legs elevated (Figure 3–8). It consists of a breathing visualization, moving sequentially through the shoulder girdle, rib cage, pelvis, and legs to encourage expansion and release in the whole body and mind. Students are then encouraged to explore vocalization in this released state, using their somatic awareness to notice and then redirect habitual patterns of tension as they arise.

Exercise

1. Lie down on a mat or firmly padded surface with a small, firm pillow or folded towel under your head so that your head is centered on your torso. Your neck should retain its soft natural curve, so it's not overly arched or flattened out. Rest your lower legs on an elevated prop (e.g., chair, ottoman) so your shins are parallel to the ceiling and your pelvis feels flat and heavy on the mat. Your legs should feel supported so the muscles can completely let go. Allow your arms to float towards the ceiling, crossing over each other in the air and then gently draping over your chest wherever they can hang without muscular tightening or holding. If this isn't comfortable, you can rest your palms on the front of your hips with elbows wide.

2. Allow the weight of your body to surrender to gravity, and notice any sensations that arise in your body or mind, without judging or trying to fix anything. Are there any areas of tension, pain, or discomfort? Where do you feel your body in contact with a surface? Do you notice differences between the two sides? Where do you feel the breath most prominently in your body?

3. Visualize the inner borders of your shoulder blades, and imagine they are gills that you could breathe

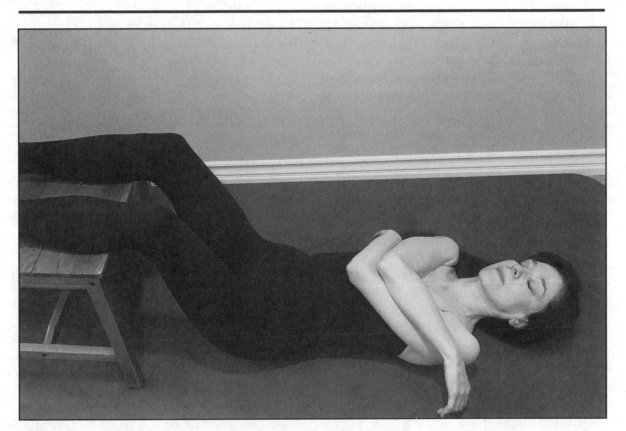

Figure 3–8. Modified constructive rest position. Photograph courtesy of Suzan Postel.

through. Inhale through these gills, allowing them to inflate your shoulder blades so they drift farther apart. On the exhale they continue opening as the upper chest softens down into the space between the shoulder blades.

4. Breathe into the upper side ribs so they spread apart like fingers opening, and on the exhale these ribs drift outward towards the sides of the room as the front ribs, heart, and lungs melt down into the space between them.

5. Inhale into the lower ribs widening all the way down and across the back of the waist, and on the exhale continue to widen as the contents of the abdomen melt downward through the back of the body.

6. Inhale past your bottom back ribs down to your sitz bones, inflating the back of your pelvis, which spreads out like a puddle on the exhale as the low belly empties through the pelvis into the ground below.

7. Inhale past the sitz bones, through your legs, down to the soles of your feet, and on the exhale visualize the weight of the legs releasing downward through the back of your pelvis, which spreads out and sinks into the earth.

8. Inhale again into all these areas: the rib cage, pelvis, and legs, and on the exhale allow the whole body to surrender to gravity, imprinting into the ground.

9. Allow your arms to drift back down by your sides with the palms up. Check in and notice if there's been any change:

Is the back of your body more in contact with the mat?

Do your collar bones and shoulder blades feel wider and farther from your ears?

Do your rib cage and pelvis feel wider and heavier on the mat?

Do you feel the movement of your breath expanding and releasing the rib cage and pelvis?

Do you feel calmer?

10. Maintaining awareness of these new sensations, try adding gentle vocalization, like sighs, humming, or lip trills. If you notice any tensions or holding patterns arising, simply invite them to release, and

begin again. You can gradually bring these explorations into standing posture and your extended singing practice.

Breath Stamina Exercise for Aging Singers

Barbara Fox DeMaio

Purpose of Exercise

■ To help rebuild breathing and vocal stamina in the aging voice
■ To encourage the use of the intercostals in breathing

Origin of Exercise

This exercise is based on exercises I learned while studying with Nancy Stokes Milnes in New York and Sergio Bertocchi in Italy.

Overview of Exercise

Aging has a profound effect on pulmonary function; the trachea softens and widens, peribronchial muscles atrophy, and pulmonary alveoli and bronchioles dilate. The alveoli also thicken and develop more capillaries, causing problems with oxygen diffusion in the lungs. Vital capacity can reduce by as much as 40% between the ages of 20 and 80, along with a deterioration of the forced expiratory volume, tensile strength, and elasticity of the lungs. Sataloff emphasized, "As lungs and thorax lose their elasticity and distensibility and abdominal muscle mass begins to deteriorate, it is all the more important for a professional voice user to be in peak physical condition." This exercise is based on the use of the intercostal muscles to allow the rib cage to stay open, keeping the diaphragm down and allowing the breath to escape in a controlled manner. The Italians call this "cantare in apnea," meaning "singing while holding the breath." Doscher says, "Considering

the variability of breathing practices, it is probably well-advised to admit that from an empirical point of view, and probably from a scientific one as well, there is no set formula for ideal breathing that will fit every singer." In other words, there are many ways to teach breath support. I have found that this method is particularly helpful for older singers who have begun to lose muscle tone and experience difficulty in singing long lines.

Exercise

To begin this exercise, take a breath and hold it gently; notice how your ribs stay out without any feeling of tension. Then, gently push with the palm of both hands or the fist of both hands on a wall or against a piano, with the hands at approximately waist level (I was taught to push against the piano, but that will not work for individuals who are taller or shorter than average). Use enough pressure so that you feel the intercostals engage and the back open almost as though there were a zipper opening the spine. Sing the exercise, starting in the lowest part of the voice, at a moderate speed. When you begin to run out of breath, start to slowly push harder on the wall, being careful to use the muscles in the back, releasing the neck and shoulders as much as possible. Then step away from the wall and attempt to recreate the feeling of support without pushing against anything. Step back to the wall and attempt to sing the exercise twice without taking a second breath. Then, once again, step away from the wall and attempt to do the same thing without pushing

on the wall. Continue to raise the pitch by half steps; however, should you start to feel tension or tiredness, stop and take a rest. The exercise should be a regular part of the warm-up routine. You should spend at least 5 to 10 minutes in every warm-up session.

References

Doscher, B. (1994). *The functional unity of the singing voice* (2nd ed., p. 25). Metuchen, NJ: Scarecrow.

Hodges, P., & Melton, J. (2010). *Breath management strategies of elite vocal performers across a range of performance genres.* Department of Physiotherapy, SHRS, University of Queensland, Brisbane, Australia.

Leden, H. v., & Alessi, D. (1994). The aging voice. In Michael Benninger, Barbara Jacobson, & Alex Johnson (Eds.), *Vocal arts medicine: The care and prevention of professional voice disorders* (p. 274). New York, NY: Thieme Medical.

Melton, J., & Tom, K. (2012). *One voice: Integrating singing and theatre voice techniques* (2nd ed.). Long Grove, IL: Waveland.

Roy, N., & Leeper, H. (1993). Effects of the manual laryngeal musculoskeletal tension reduction technique as a treatment for functional voice disorders: Perceptual and acoustic measures. *Journal of Voice, 7*(3), 242–249.

Sapienza, C., & Hoffman Ruddy, B. (2012). *Voice disorders.* San Diego, CA: Plural Publishing.

Sataloff, R. T., Spiegel, J., & Caputo Rosen, D. (1991). The effects of age on the voice. In Robert T. Sataloff (Ed.), *Professional voice: The science and art of clinical care* (p. 265). New York, NY: Raven Press.

Notes

4

Stretching and Relaxation for Tongue and Jaw

Jaw Exercises for Singing

Miriam van Mersbergen

Purpose of Exercise

■ Gain awareness of the contribution of jaw tension during singing
■ Reduce postural tension of the muscles of the jaw

Origin of Exercise

Sometimes having a tight jaw is so habitual that we are unaware of the degree of tension. Jaw tension has been known to interfere with optimal resonance, tightness in the muscles of the face and neck, and laryngeal adduction. Furthermore, sometimes singing with inefficient technique can lead a singer to overuse the jaw muscles and stress them. Managing jaw tension will help avoid running into jaw problems in the future. These massages come from a larger set of massages for the face and jaw adapted from neuromuscular therapy techniques of Paul St. John.

Overview of Exercise

One way to note if you have jaw tension that might interfere with voicing is to find a favorite exercise, passage, or lick that you frequently use. Sing it a couple of times. Then perform the following jaw massages on each side of your face. Sing the exercise, passage, or lick again and note if you feel a better sense of placement, flexibility, or intonation. Knowing how much jaw tension can affect singing is a good motivation to engage in jaw massage daily and practice good jaw hygiene (listed below).

Exercise

There are four basic jaw muscles. Two are easily accessed from the outside of the mouth, the masseter and temporalis muscles; two are deep within the muscles of the face, the medial and lateral pterygoids, but their insertions can be accessed from the outside. Sit with your head supported against a wall to facilitate a relaxed neck posture and good spinal alignment.

Masseter Muscle

Support the opposite side of your head with your entire hand from the same side (Figure 4–1).

Figure 4–1. Masseter muscle—Step 1. Photograph courtesy of Regina Dentzman.

With your thumb from the other hand, glide down from the cheek bone to the jaw line around the angle of the jaw (Figure 4-2).

Do this four or five times, moving back toward your ear.

Now using your index finger from the same hand, find the back of the upper cheek bone (Figure 4-3).

Using short sweeps, glide across the lower part of your cheek bone toward your nose.

Do this four or five times.

Temporalis Muscle

Support the opposite side of your head with your entire hand from the same side. With your first and second finger from the other hand, find the temporalis muscle (the fan-like muscle on your temples and adjacent hairline), gently use a circular motion, and begin massaging upward from the level of the eye (Figure 4-4).

Fan outward to cover the entire muscle.

Do this for 10 to 15 times.

With short strokes, glide across the tendon fibers above the cheek bones (Figure 4-5).

Do this four or five times.

Open the mouth slightly and glide across the fibers below the cheek bones.

Medial Pterygoid Muscle

Support the opposite side of your head with your entire hand from the same side.

Hook your index finger from the other hand underneath the back part of the corner of the jaw (Figure 4-6).

Glide inward four or five times.

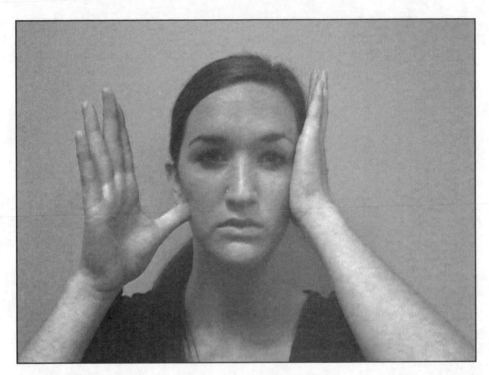

Figure 4–2. Masseter muscle—Step 2. Photograph courtesy of Regina Dentzman.

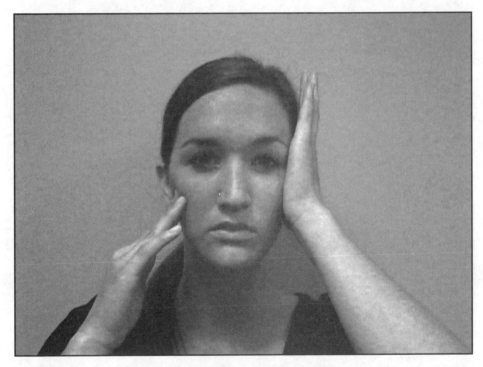

Figure 4–3. Masseter muscle—Step 3. Photograph courtesy of Regina Dentzman.

Figure 4–4. Temporalis muscle—Step 1. Photograph courtesy of Regina Dentzman.

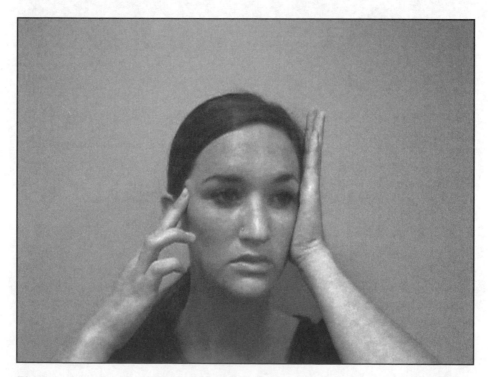

Figure 4–5. Temporalis muscle—Step 2. Photograph courtesy of Regina Dentzman.

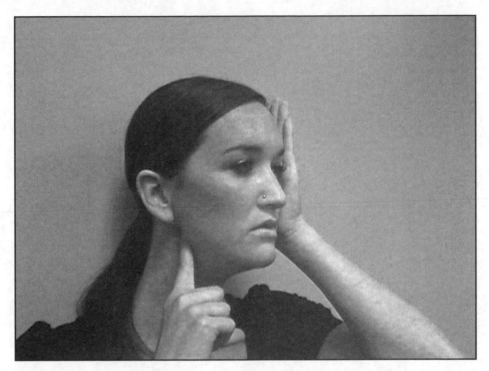

Figure 4–6. Medial pterygoid muscle. Photograph courtesy of Regina Dentzman.

Lateral Pterygoid Muscle

Support the opposite side of your head with your entire hand from the same side.

With your mouth slightly open, find the jaw hinge (condyle) right in front of the tragus of the ear.

Pressing rather firmly with your first and second finger, move up and down without gliding.

Do this four or five times.

To maneuver around the masseter muscle, you might want to move the jaw slightly to the opposite side to find a deeper muscle (Figure 4–7).

For a deeper massage, these muscles can be accessed from the inside of your mouth by a trained massage therapist or speech-language pathologist.

Jaw Opening/Tongue Tension Isolation

Miriam van Mersbergen

Purpose of Exercise

- Facilitate relaxed back of tongue during jaw opening
- Gain awareness of the relationship between tension in the jaw and tongue and tension in the larynx

Origin of Exercise

We are often told that opening the jaw is helpful in obtaining a louder sound. However, we have reflexes in our tongue that want to pull the tongue back (retract) when the jaw opens. So, here is an exercise that helps

Figure 4–7. Lateral pterygoid muscle. Photograph courtesy of Regina Dentzman.

dissociate the jaw opening from tongue retraction. It also heightens our awareness about how our mouth structures affect the feeling of how we sing.

Overview of Exercise

This exercise is best performed during a resonant hum. Resonant humming is much like a meditation hum or chanting hum. The tone should be unaffected and relaxed, almost on a sigh. In this way, we are working on the most fundamental and basic vocal sound, without interference from a lot of style and performance requirements.

Exercise

With your mouth closed, hum in an easy, mid-low pitch. During this hum, you will want to glide up and down

---

Jaw Hygiene

Reducing habits that overstress the jaw:

- Gum chewing
- Nail biting
- Chewing ice
- Over-opening the mouth during yawning
- Over-opening the mouth to bite food
- Leaning on your jaw with your hands
- Clenching at night (bruxism)
- Clenching during the day due to stress
- Poor neck posture with a jutting jaw, putting stress on the joint

Promoting habits that maintain optimal relaxation and posture:

- Ice and hot packs on the jaw if fatigued
- Daily massages and stretches

between a half-step and a minor third. Keeping your mouth closed, drop your jaw so that there is ample space between your molars. You could describe this as a dopey look to the face. Note how the hum changes properties and resonances. Do this for about 1 to 2 minutes.

Next, do the same exercise, but this time, place your tongue along the outside of your top teeth (cheek side) near the back molars on one side. The tongue should be stretched back as if you are cleaning something out of the top back molar. Hum again in the same way with the jaw dropped. Note how the properties of the hum change this time in terms of how much pressing and force it takes to make a reasonable sound. Do this for 1 to 2 minutes.

You may want to hum back and forth between the basic jaw drop and the jaw drop with tongue stretch to highlight your sensations. Remember to breathe between every trial and start with a new sound each time.

Reducing Jaw Region Tension and Cramping

Walt Fritz

Purpose of Exercise

To become familiar with patterns of jaw region tension, fatigue, and discomfort, and provide remediation through a sustained and gentle self-stretching.

Origin of Exercise

This exercise was originally taught to me in my myofascial release (manual therapy) training in the early 1990s, one targeting the patient populations of physical therapists. Through modifications in its application, the technique has become more applicable to the needs of the singer and vocal performer.

From a personal perspective, I found this self-treatment sequence particularly useful in reducing the jaw cramping that I had noticed while eating firmer

food. During the course of eating a bagel, I frequently had to stop for "rests" to allow the cramping in my jaw to diminish. The rest time would reduce the cramping, allowing me to eat a bit more of the bagel until I needed another rest. In hindsight, I had similar difficulties when speaking in public for extended periods, especially with more emotionally charged situations, such as in my role as an educator. This combined activity of speaking to a group of professional peers was both a physical experience as well as an emotional challenge, one in which I previously had difficulty with marked fatigue in the jaw region and elsewhere. After self-treating myself in the following area, my experience was greatly improved. I still on occasion need to provide myself a "tune-up," but as this area has been explored through touch, as well as becoming more comfortable in the public education realm, my negative experiences have significantly lessened.

Overview of Exercise

This exercise involves placing one finger inside the mouth, between the outer aspect of the back upper molars and inside of the back of the jaw. Very light pressures are used throughout with no aggressiveness. Plan on spending 5 to 10 minutes daily for a period of a few days or longer. More than just a rote stretch, following a protocol, as you place a finger in the desired location, you should be able to replicate familiar aspects of your fatigue, cramping, or discomfort.

When to Do This Exercise

Timing tends not to matter, so it may be advantageous to do when you are not rushed. While frequency is also not crucial, most people tend to benefit from once daily stretching for a period of at least a few days.

Exercise

This exercise is presented in a way that closely matches the manner in which I use it in treatment. Individual adaptations and modifications should matter little. I teach a style of treatment (and self-treatment) that relies strongly on the patient (you) to decide what is both relevant and potentially beneficial, which may conflict with thoughts that the clinician knows what is best. When I treat (or teach self-treatment), the primary goal is often to get my patient to replicate familiar sensations, which in the case of the jaw might be cramping, fatigue, or other sensations. I will ask that you do the same thing; when you place your finger inside your mouth, you should be seeking to replicate familiar feelings. Once replicated, you will simply stay in contact with that area, providing very gentle pressures (stretch) until the sensations dissipate. You may feel the area soften, get warm, or many other experiences, but the goal is a less negative sensation, whether in the moment or during activity.

First, a look at the anatomy of the area. The maxilla bone encases the upper teeth, while the mandibular bone encases the lower teeth. You will be inserting your finger into the area between your upper back outside molars and the inner aspect of your mandible/jaw bone. I prefer to have you position your index finger so that the nail is in contact with the upper teeth,

leaving your finger pad to come into contact with the inner mandible. Figure 4-8 shows how to hold your hand and finger. In that photo, the model is stretching the left side of her mouth. To access the right side of the mouth, switch hands. Figure 4-9 shows the location of finger placement on the skull model. Figure 4-10 shows the model with the index finger in the self-treatment position.

- To best access this region, place your moistened index finger, nail facing toward the upper teeth and parallel with the upper teeth throughout the technique as if you are following the line of the upper teeth back toward the back of your head.
- If you are trying to stretch the left side of the jaw, you will be using your right hand. You will turn your hand so that the fingernail is facing toward your face and the finger pad is facing away from your face (see Figure 4-9).
- Keep your nail in contact with the teeth and slide it back until you meet mild resistance, which you

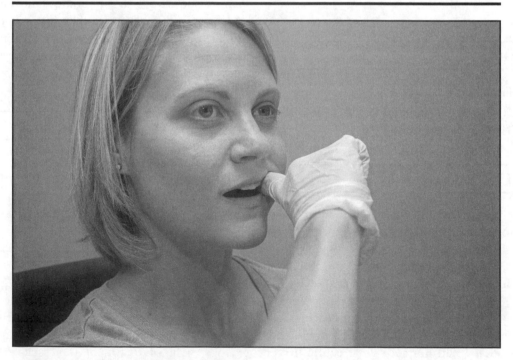

Figure 4–8. Hand and finger position.

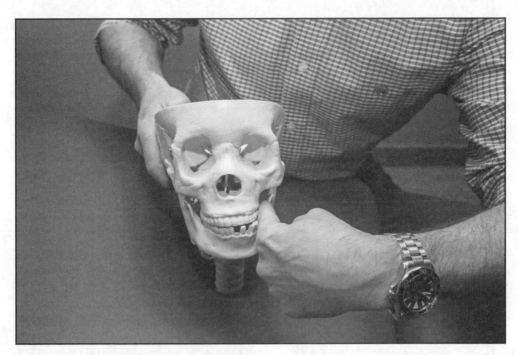

Figure 4–9. Finger placement.

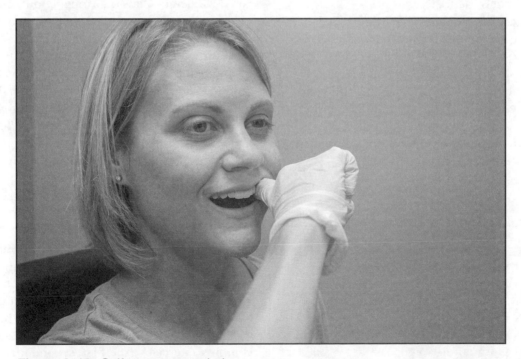

Figure 4–10. Self-treatment technique.

will feel with the pad of the index finger. This resistance on the pad side of your finger is from the contact with the inner part of the mandible.

- With your nail in connection with the back teeth and your finger pad in contact with the inner jaw, if you tried to push back toward the back of the mouth, you will feel like you are trying to open a gap. Don't push hard, stay lightly in contact with a small amount of pressure.
- At this point, ask yourself, "What do I feel? Is there a familiar sensation of tightness, fatigue, or other?" You are seeking to replicate a familiar feeling or sensation and if it feels like you are pushing too hard, back off a bit. Lighter pressures can be just as effective as more aggressive pressures.
- If you can replicate your familiar negative sensation, then stay lightly engaged with pressure on this area, allowing the region to stretch and relax. You may notice that your finger seems to move more deeply into that gap. Continue with this stretch for a few minutes or until you are fatigued.
- If you fail to replicate familiar sensations, you may need to move your finger, exploring other areas. If you are unable to reproduce familiar tightness and the stretch feels ineffective, stop.
- After stretching through this particular region, allow your index finger to move into the cheek area, just forward of where the finger pad hit the jaw bone, slowly stretching to find regions of familiar tightness, etc. If found, apply the same very gentle, sustained stretch until the tension eases.
- Rest and then repeat on the other side, switching hands.

Disclaimer: Please do not use this information as a substitute for medical advice. A proper medical diagnosis and clearance should always be obtained from your physician before engaging in self-treatment. Do not perform if open sores or wounds are present, if your sensation is impaired, or if excessive pain is present with finger placement in the mouth region.

Tongue Stretches for Singers

Maria Cristina A. Jackson-Menaldi

Purpose of Exercise

- To reduce tension of the base of the tongue and get the image to reduce retraction during phonation.
- Increase forward resonance.

Origin of Exercise

As with any exercise that we use today with professional singers or actors, these are in some way ideas borrowed from other well-known techniques from the world or our own experience working with professional voice users. Tongue out exercise has been used for centuries in European singing techniques from the seventeenth to the twentieth centuries. The French technique, the Mauran technique by baritone Jean Mauran (vibration of vowels behind front teeth), and Madeleine Mansion (tongue out exercise) has been used in France and is well known all over the world. This exercise is a modified exercise that I have been using for years in South America, Europe, and the United States. Those techniques have been very well known in South America, especially when I was studying music and choir direction. Also, later working as a voice pathologist in the Opera Theater "Teatro Colon" in Buenos Aires, Argentina, those techniques were very popular among singers and singing teachers.

Overview of Exercise

The exercise is my own combination, which consists of pulling the tongue out of the mouth and down the same way that a laryngologist sees the vocal fold using a rigid scope. The singer needs to take a quiet breath first and produce a sound forward with /hee/, one-half a tone and a tone like C, C#, C progressing to more complex exercises (see first, second, third variations below). Utterances of the tongue out with this sound reduces tension at the back of the mouth and base of the tongue, and at the same time reduces retraction of the tongue. Singers should feel relaxed and open after completing this exercise.

Producing the vibration of the /hee/ sound behind the upper teeth generates what we call the "Mauran point," helping to get more forward sound later when singing.

Exercise

1. Sit in a relaxed posture in a chair or standing with good alignment.
   a. Make sure to align your body with a relaxed face, neck, shoulder, upper back, and chest.
   b. Use diaphragmatic breathing.
2. Take your tongue out of the mouth with a gauze, one hand or two, as in Figure 4–11.
   a. Take a relaxing silent breath.
   b. Produce a /hee/ sound C, C#, and so on. Adapt the starting notes for a male or female vocal range. Increase complexity as the singer becomes comfortable with exercise.
3. Let the tongue rest comfortably inside of your mouth.
4. Initiate a fake yawn to open and stretch the back of the mouth.
5. Do a lip vibration up and down and say any sentence.
   a. Singer should feel full open sensation of the tongue and sound free and forward.
6. Speak short phrases with this new sense of opening immediately following the exercises ended, or try to sing.
7. Complete the exercise once or twice throughout the day before performances or rehearsals, when tension/strain is felt in the back of the tongue.

Figure 4–11. Tongue stretch.

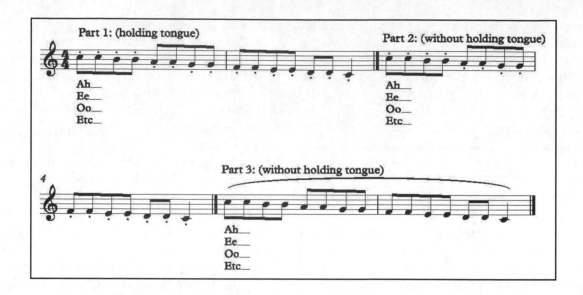

Staccato and Legato Tongue Release

Tracy Bourne

Purpose of Exercise

- To coordinate simultaneous onset of breath and phonation
- To identify and prevent tongue root tension
- To build awareness of a relaxed vocal tract in staccato and legato phrases
- To encourage efficient vocalization

Origin of Exercise

Richard Miller has written about the benefits of building a coordinated onset in the classical voice. This exercise adapts Miller's work for a music theatre context, where the tongue is generally required to be more forward and in a more "speech-like" position. The exercise also builds on the work of Jeannette LoVetri, who has written about the contemporary commercial music (CCM) mix voice in which "chest" and "head" registers tend to transition at a higher pitch than classical vocal styles, generally between F4 and C5.

Overview of Exercise

This is an exercise that supports the development of mix voice in a music theatre context. It assumes that the voice is well warmed up and that "chest" (modal) and "head" (falsetto) vocal registers have been exercised separately. The exercise should be sung in the lower middle range of the voice, and then modulated by semitone or tone to the highest comfortable range of the voice. The exercise is most appropriate for the developing intermediate singer and for singers with poor vocal onset (i.e., glottal or breathy) or a tendency to pull the tongue back into the mouth while singing (tongue root tension).

Exercise

Part One: Identification of Tongue Release

1. Project the tongue out of the mouth, a little farther than the bottom teeth, and hold with the thumb and two fingers. Do not grip the tongue too tightly: Holding the tip of the tongue is intended to "remind" the posterior body of the tongue to remain high and forward.
2. Take in a comfortable breath, ensuring that the abdomen is released during inhalation. The inhalation should not be audible.

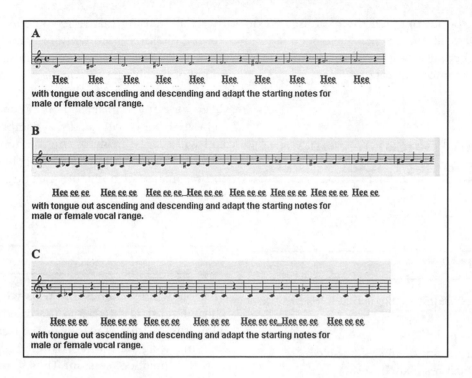

3. Choose a key in the singer's lower middle range; possibly A major for women, C major for men.

4. On a comfortable vowel, vocalize a descending octave scale with two staccato notes per pitch. Ensure the staccato is performed with simultaneous onset rather than breathy or glottal onset. (Less advanced students might do better to sing a descending 5th scale.)

5. While singing, ensure that the tongue remains forward rather than pulling back into the mouth.

Part Two: Maintaining Tongue Release

1. Allow the tongue to sit inside the mouth, with the tip touching the bottom teeth. The singer will imagine the posterior of the tongue is in the same position as it was in Part One of this exercise.

2. Take in a comfortable breath, ensuring that the abdomen is released during inhalation. The inhalation should not be audible.

3. In the same key, and on the same vowel as in Part One, vocalize a descending octave scale with two staccato notes per pitch. Ensure the staccato is performed with simultaneous onset rather than breathy

or glottal onset. The posterior of the tongue should remain in the higher, more forward position.

4. If the singer notices excessive tongue or vocal tract tension, or an inappropriate onset (glottal or breathy), then he or she should return to Part One of the exercise.

Part Three: Legato with Tongue Release

1. Allow the tongue to sit inside the mouth, with the tip touching the bottom teeth. The singer will imagine the posterior of the tongue is in the same position as it was in Part One of the exercise.

2. Take in a comfortable breath, ensuring that the abdomen is released during inhalation. The inhalation should not be audible.

3. In the same key, and on the same vowel as in Parts One and Two, sing a descending scale on a legato phrase with one note per pitch. Note that the posterior of the tongue should remain in the higher and more forward position of Parts One and Two.

4. If the singer notices excessive tongue or vocal tract tension, then he or she should return to Part One of the exercise.

The singer should practice the exercises on different vowels. Once all three stages have been satisfactorily accomplished, the singer can modulate up to a higher key, by a semitone or tone.

Increasing Vocal Resonance by Decreasing Facial Tension

Catherine A. Walker

Purpose of Exercises

- To release tension in the nasolabial folds or "smile" lines
- To release tension in lips
- To release tension in the cheek muscles
- To increase vocal resonance

Origin of Exercises

It is universally accepted that lip position in singing has an impact on the amount of brightness or twang present in the vocal tone. Furthermore, lip position is key to stylistic authenticity as well as the creation of certain vowels. Experience has shown, however, that this is only part of the story. Another consideration is the *condition or quality* of the muscles in the lip and face. Are they overly tightened, under-energized, or optimally engaged for the task at hand? Regardless of how well someone is singing at the source, overly tightened facial and lip musculature can impact the overall resonance of the voice. The question is, why? Overtones are present in every sound we make and through practice and manipulation they can be magnified, diminished, or completely muted. By magnifying overtones, the voice will sound fuller, louder, and more resonant. Conversely, if they are muted, the voice will sound thinner and less resonant. This is analogous to the function of a damper pedal on a piano. Try playing a single note on a high-quality piano. If the damper pedal is depressed while playing the note, the vibrations from that pitch will sympathetically activate the overtones from all the related strings,

therefore causing that note to sound more resonant. Playing the same note without damper pedal engagement will result in fewer overtones, so the tone will sound noticeably less resonant and less full and might even sound softer. The lips and the muscles of the face work in a similar fashion. When they are overly tightened, they will act as a damper for the voice and will silence many of the overtones which could enhance the vocal tone and will therefore minimize the resonance of both the speaking and the singing voice.

Overview of Exercises

The following stretches and trills will help to release chronic tension patterns in the face and lips and will allow the overtones to ring more freely. They can be helpful during the warm-up routine as well as throughout the practice session. These exercises can be applied across a singer's entire range using a variety of vowels and diverse styles of repertoire. They are helpful to singers of all ages and experience levels. It is especially useful for beginning singers to develop optimal habits from the very beginning rather than requiring correction later.

Exercises

Locating and Releasing the Smile or Laugh Lines

The **nasolabial folds** are the two **folds** of skin that run from the side of each nostril to the corner of the mouth. They separate the cheeks from the upper lip. The folds are composed of muscles and bundles of fibrous tissue which can be extremely impactful to the singer's tone. Releasing or optimizing the smile muscles will allow more overtones to ring and will therefore increase vocal resonance.

1. To release the nasolabial folds, begin by using your right index finger, gently trace a line from the outside of your right nostril to the right corner of your mouth (Figure 4–12). It is common for singers to have very defined muscles in

Figure 4–12. Identifying nasolabial folds.

this area. Additionally, many voice teachers use prompts such as "bite the apple lips" and the "inner smile" to facilitate a lift in the facial muscles. Of course, these are valid prompts; however, if taken to an extreme they can become counterproductive. Regardless of the origin, the result is that many singers have overly tightened nasolabial folds, which in turn impact their tone quality and vocal resonance.

2. For the next step, wash your hands thoroughly or use a latex glove. Begin to release this area by firmly pinching and holding the muscles between your thumb and index finger. First place your index finger at the base of your nostril and then slide your thumb up inside your mouth to meet it. Firmly press your two fingers toward each other and hold for 30 seconds. Begin this process at the corner of the nostril (Figure 4-13) and then repeat as you slowly work your way down the fold till you reach the corner of the mouth (Figure 4-14).

3. Repeat this sequence while singing. This will often yield surprising and dramatic results.

Lip Stretches and Cheek Trills

It is also important to evaluate the amount of tension in the lips. In more contemporary styles, the lips are in a more horizontal position. Many singers in an effort to spread their lips actually draw the lips tightly over their teeth. Once again, this will impact the presence of overtones. The lips can remain soft and supple regardless of position.

Figure 4–13. Releasing nasolabial folds.

Figure 4–14. Releasing nasolabial folds.

1. Firmly hold the top lip and stretch it forward and hold for 30 seconds (Figure 4–15).
2. Firmly hold your cheeks and stretch them forward and hold for 30 seconds (Figure 4–16).
3. Firmly hold the bottom lip and stretch it forward and hold for 30 seconds (Figure 4–17).
4. Repeat each of the above stretches while vocalizing. Observe which of these has the most impact. It will vary with each singer depending on her/his use patterns.

Cheek Trills

Since all the muscles of the face are interconnected, it is worth spending time releasing tension in the cheeks.

1. Gently nestle the back of your right hand on your right cheek just under the cheekbone, fingers pointing toward and just touching the lips with your fingers (Figure 4–18).
2. Keeping lips together, exhale on the left side of the mouth, trilling the cheek muscles as well as the left side of the lips.
3. This should feel quite different from a simple, centralized lip trill, where the cheeks remain quiet.
4. Repeat on the other side.
5. You may notice one side will trill more easily than the other. All our physical patterns of use are asymmetrical to greater and lesser degrees.
6. This can help rebalance the muscles of the face, so they can respond more freely helping to optimize the voice.

Figure 4–15. Top lip stretch.

Figure 4–16. Cheek stretch.

Figure 4–17. Bottom lip stretch.

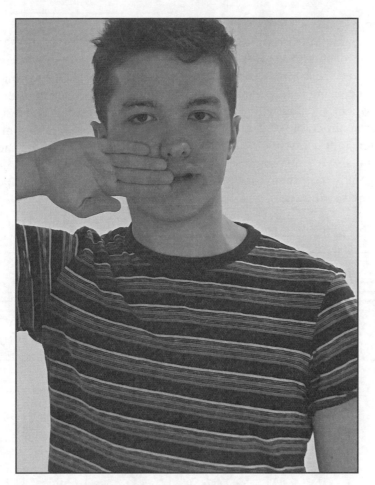

Figure 4–18. Hand on cheek.

Guy-La Tongue Release and Flexibility

Edrie Means Weekly

Purpose of Exercise

■ To loosen the anterior and posterior tongue
■ To separate and isolate tongue activity
■ To promote tongue flexibility
■ To promote positive effect on technical outcome impacting the function of the tongue

Origin of Exercise

This is an exercise I have developed based on a "chewy" exercise my own voice teacher, Van Lawrence Award recipient, Dr. Janette Ogg, used.

Overview of Exercise

Often tongue tension manifests itself in the muscle bearing down on the larynx, putting pressure on the vocal folds. There are all sorts of tongue exercises, vowel shaping, and vowel distortion shaping exercises to support CCM repertoire. This is another exercise designed to loosen the tongue and promote tongue flexibility through isolation of the posterior and anterior tongue actions. This exercise is intended for early on in warming up the voice, using light phonation on a five-note scale as shown in the following musical notation. The jaw must remain stable and not move. The tongue must function independently of the jaw. This will be useful in various styles needing resonance changes where singers greatly vary their tone quality by altering the shape of the vocal tract.

Exercise

1. Opening the mouth to the size of a cork while keeping the jaw in a comfortable and healthy position will decrease tension. The tongue should be loose, relaxed, flat, and forward, with the tip resting lightly behind the bottom teeth. The jaw must remain stable throughout the exercise and not move. Figure 4–19 shows the singer using her index finger gently on her chin to remind her not to move her jaw.

Guy-la, Guy-la, Guy-la, Guy-la, Guy-la, Guy-la, Guy.

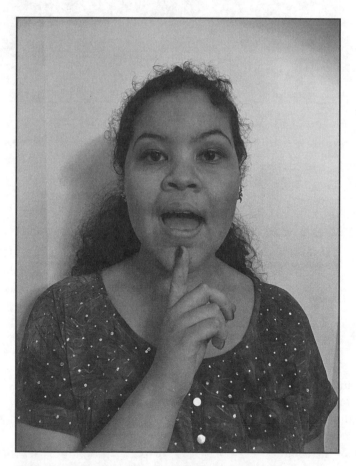

Figure 4–19. Using finger to stabilize the jaw.

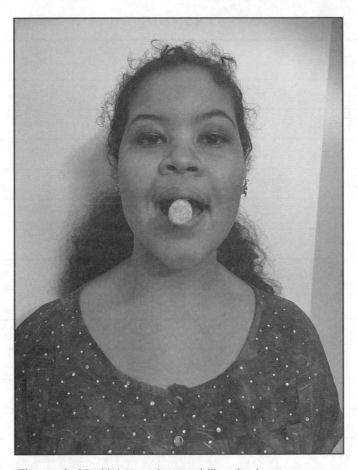

Figure 4–20. Using cork to stabilize the jaw.

An alternative method is to have the student use a cork to stabilize the jaw, as is shown in Figure 4–20.

2. Use a five-tone scale pattern beginning on the fifth with the starting fifth being G4 for women and G3 for men. Move up the keyboard by half steps until the fifth is D5 for women and D4 for men. At any time during the exercise, if the singer is experiencing any jaw tension, stop the exercise and reduce jaw tension by gently massaging the jaw muscles.

3. With light phonation and with a stable jaw, begin with the stop plosive consonant [G], which causes a posterior tongue lift touching the soft palate, followed by the diphthong [aI], while the tip of the tongue remains behind the back of the bottom front teeth.

The tip of the tongue rises to the alveolar ridge, located on the hard palate behind the upper front teeth and flips through on [la].

Reference

Jackson-Menaldi, M. C. (2002). *La voz patológica*. Buenos Aires, Argentina: Editorial Médica Panamericana.

Notes

SECTION II

Training the Hybrid Singer

Introduction and Overview

Given the varied demands placed on contemporary commercial music (CCM) performers, the vocal athlete must navigate multiple levels of fitness, ranging from general physical fitness to a high level of vocal fitness in order to meet industry demands and performance expectations in a competitive arena. Although there are multiple CCM vocal styles, all require a strong, stable vocal mechanism that is balanced and efficient.

Chapter 17 of *The Vocal Athlete, Second Edition* text, "Exercise Physiology Principles for Training the Vocal Athlete," discusses the importance of training and conditioning the vocal mechanism required to meet the demands needed for CCM vocal styles. Just as the professional athlete has coaches and trainers implementing exercise physiology principles to maximize performance and minimize injury, so too must the vocal athlete use warm-ups, cool-downs, and strengthening exercises to ensure career longevity and vocal health. Section II highlights exercises which are helpful for vocal warm up to calibrate the vocal mechanism for more technical training. Additionally, we have included exercises which can help promote cooling down at the end of intense performance, and/or recalibrating and releasing vocal tension that occur as a result of intensive voice use. Chapters 6 and 7 focus on exercises generally aimed at fostering strength and coordination, thus preparing the singer for more rigorous vocal tasks. This section concludes with exercises aimed at training specific vocal styles and specialty populations.

Chapter 5: Vocal Warm-Ups and Cool-Downs

The physiologic benefits of vocal warm-up and cool-down are discussed in Chapter 17 of *The Vocal Athlete, Second Edition*. Although studies looking at the benefit of vocal warm-up have had varied results, and CCM vocal styles are not typically represented in these studies, warming up generally constitutes a part of the traditional voice lesson. As mentioned in the beginning of this book, an exercise is only as effective as the intention behind it. In exercise science, the goal of physical warm-up is to increase blood flow and oxygen to muscles, and to promote flexibility and range of motion of muscles. Runners must stretch and warm up before a race, and so too must the vocal athlete prepare the vocal mechanism for more rigorous work. Additionally, the runner is not likely to simply cease running at the end of the race, rather he will gradually slow the pace down to a jog, then a walk before stretching his muscles again when he is done. Vocal cool-down exercises can be thought of as a means to "neutralize" the vocal mechanism after technical work, promoting "active recovery" from athletic singing. The concept of vocal cool-down should not be overlooked, especially when the singer has been singing actively at increased volumes and pitch range. Recall from Chapter 1 in *The Vocal Athlete, Second Edition* that muscles work in agonist/antagonist pairs—meaning that when one muscle is highly active, its antagonist muscle is less active and vice versa. This phenomenon is referred to as reciprocal inhibition. As an example, if a singer has engaged in an extended period of singing at high intensity in the chest register (the thyroarytenoid [TA] muscle is presumed to be more active relative to its partner, the cricothyroid [CT] muscle), it makes sense to engage the opposite register as part of the vocal cool-down. Therefore, light vocalization in head register, where CT is highly active relative to TA, in a descending pattern all the way down into the low range will facilitate relaxation of the TA muscle and help return the voice to a more neutral default setting. Conversely, if working extensively in the head register for an extended period of time, the vocal cool-down routine should also include some light chest register. The same principle may also be applied to various character voices requiring exaggerated placement and brightness. For example, some characters may require a very high laryngeal position and forward tongue placement to achieve a certain character voice (i.e., Sally in the Charlie Brown cartoons, Adelaide in *Guys and Dolls*). In this scenario, the vocal cool-down may incorporate exercise promoting a lowered larynx combined with back, rounded vowels to help maintain balance. In essence, the cool-down exercises are intended to downshift the vocal mechanism and prevent it from getting stuck in a default setting or gear.

The exercises in this chapter can be thought of and used as vocal warm-ups to calibrate the voice prior to more active, technical vocal work, and several can be used as vocal cool-down exercises to return the vocal instrument to a neutral state after use. Singers and teachers should incorporate various exercises into their routine based on need. While not scientifically studied in a rigorous manner, empirical evidence in our studios and clinical settings indicate that vocal cool-down exercises are beneficial for restoring a more neutral vocal "gear" helping to minimize fatigue and hasten rebound to normal status.

In general, use of tongue or lip trills can be very useful to expand into the upper pitch ranges lightly and easily. Dr. Caroline Helton's motorboat exercise provides a gentle warm-up to gently engage the breath while relaxing the tongue and jaw musculature during low intensity vocalization. Dr. Norman Spivey describes a standard descending five-tone scale on a lip trill moving to a vowel for establishing precise coordination of airflow and onset of sound. This exercise, when used in the midrange (speaking range) can also

be used to execute finding a resonant voice placement. Beverly Patton describes a warm-up exercise for the midrange using a phrase first on an interval of 3rd, then 5th, then octave. By increasing her interval distance, the exercise becomes technically more difficult. The second phase of her exercise begins to incorporate the belting warm-up. The Estill inspired "mirening" exercise described by Tom Burke uses a semi-occluded vocal tract to promote a comfortable, bright, and stable sound. Collum, Dunn, and Hoffman Ruddy introduce a Linklater-based palate lift exercise to bring awareness to the effects of palatal movement on sound quality. This exercise can be used as either a warm-up or cool-down in addition to working through challenging, technical portions of repertoire. Jennifer Muckala uses a gargle technique to simultaneously condition the voice for active use and endurance throughout the vocal range while deactivating extrinsic musculature and extraneous laryngeal, jaw, and tongue musculature during active singing. This exercise also may serve as vocal cool-down. The blowfish exercise described by Marci Rosenberg uses inflated cheeks to create a sense of back pressure and release in the vocal tract. This exercise is helpful as both a vocal warm up/calibrator and as a cool down. Kari Ragan provides a useful semi-occluded vocal tract cool-down exercise. Finally, Dr. Renee Gottliebson describes a three-step exercise to cool down the voice, facilitating active recovery after rigorous singing. There are numerous variations of the above exercises that can be very effective as a vocal warm-up or cool-down exercise, and there are additional exercises that have been categorized in other chapters that can also serve as a vocal warm-up or cool-down. Singers are encouraged to try multiple variations to see what works well for their instrument.

Chapter 6: Laryngeal Strength and Coordination

Chapter 6 includes a collection of exercises to facilitate laryngeal coordination, flexibility, and strength, which are essential for healthy singing. In general, these would refer to exercises focused on developing the head register and chest register independently, in addition to stamina and agility exercises. These skills are the foundation for any style of singing and certainly for many CCM styles, particularly those that include belting. Agility and flexibility are also important components of general vocal fitness and become particularly relevant for certain CCM styles that require "riffing." These skills are particularly relevant for the hybrid singer, who must have vocal facility with multiple styles in order to be hired within the commercial market. However, even the singer who only sings in one style still must have coordination, strength, and flexibility across the entire vocal mechanism in order to reduce risk of injury and increase longevity of one's vocal career. Several of the exercises in subsequent chapters on registration and belting require the singer to have solid facility with both head voice and chest voice before working on mix or high-level belting. The exercises included in this chapter should be thought of as training and conditioning exercises to better prepare the vocal mechanism for more rigorous technical style work that is also happening during vocal training.

Stephanie Samaras begins with an exercise to move from chest to head voice and vice versa. She emphasizes connecting to the breath and controlling amount of exhalation as you transfer from head to chest and back. Clari-Bees are described by Katherine McConville as exercises aimed to strengthen vocal fold closure and improve clarity for more stable and efficient CCM singing. Mary Saunders Barton describes the *messa di voce* exercise as a balancing and coordination exercise specifically for music theater singing. Cup phonation by Marci Rosenberg is introduced as a semi-occluded vocal tract exercise using a standard Styrofoam cup allowing for production of connected sounds and different vowels while still benefiting from the resistance of the cup. It is included in this section as an exercise to train coordination of the level of vocal fold closure and airflow across the vocal range; however, this exercise is also effective as a vocal warm-up or cool-down in addition to a lower-level strengthening exercise. Throughout the centuries, *messa di voce* exercises have been used as one of the gold standards for technical excellence. Jonelyn Langenstein and Brian Petty's exercise facilitates exploration and expansion of the whistle register for both the female and the male voice. Dr. Amelia Rollings describes a vocal fry exercise, which can be used to balance vocal fold closure.

Chapter 7: Registration and Vocal Tract Modification

Registration and vocal tract modification are the primary foci of this chapter. Use of registration is one of the primary characteristics distinguishing many of the CCM styles from classical singing and the second edition of *The Vocal Athlete, Second Edition* now includes a chapter entitled Perceptions, Aesthetics & Registration in the Commercial Vocal Athlete. In order to be hireable in a commercial market, musical theater singers are required to sing well in a variety of styles that require development and balance of head register, chest register, and mix register, hence they must be hybrid singers. Register balance and development require stability and strength across the entire instrument. The true hybrid singer must be able to transition from a pop rock musical to a traditional vocal style depending on what the job or work requires, therefore vocal training must be specific to this level of adaptability.

One of the more challenging vocal skills for many singers to master is efficient use of the mix register for the purpose of a commercial music sound. Therefore, many of the exercises contributed for this chapter specifically target the mix register. A true balanced mixed voice often takes time and patience to cultivate and train. Readers will note that many of the exercises use glides as a training mechanism. Slow, controlled glides through passaggio areas allow the muscles to coordinate, strengthen, and adjust over a period of time. There may be instances where a chest-dominant mix is required and times when a head-dominant mix is needed. An important point is made by several of the authors to allow the voice to be "unstable" when training to smooth transition areas. This is counterintuitive to many singers, but this instability is an important phase in development of this vocal skillset. If the singer overrides this instability during training and engages too much muscular effort, a muscle tension pattern may result and the specificity principle discussed in Chapter 17 of *The Vocal Athlete, Second Edition* is not employed. Therefore, a true, balanced mix is never fully targeted or developed. Time and patience are often the keys when training this type of skill. As a reminder, none of the exercises in this book should cause pain, tension, or strain.

Dr. Sarah Maines begins this chapter with a head voice stability exercise with emphasis on maintaining light head voice in a descending pattern through the middle range. She uses this exercise with young female singers with weak head voice or in chest dominant singers with underdeveloped head register. Beverly Patton also describes using head register primarily in the female passaggio or in male falsetto range. She notes this exercise is to increase stamina in the midrange. Dr. Kathryn Green describes an exercise for males, head-dominant mix moving to chest-dominant mix for some of the more contemporary pop/rock music theater styles requiring this type of falsetto. Green's second exercise expands the male head voice into the upper range, while also encouraging "riffing" and ornamentation. Martin Spencer's three-part exercise uses glides to facilitate smooth transition through the passaggio with emphasis on adequate airflow and remediation of harsh vocal fold closure patterns. Michelle Rosen introduces an exercise to facilitate light chest mix. She has modified a traditional arpeggio exercise to a more CCM style. She notes that she uses this exercise in a voice lesson after working the singer independently in head and chest register. Dr. Norman Spivey also uses arpeggios in a speech-like manner to increase the range of the speech-like registration. Dr. Bari Hoffman Ruddy and Adam Lloyd describe sustained interval glides to facilitate smooth register transitions and increase vocal stamina and balance muscle function through transitions. Jeannette LoVetri presents a useful method to access the mix register by using a speaking quality as the grounding point using octave glides to expand the singer's speech quality into the higher range without strain or effort. Mary Saunders Barton also addresses vocalizing in the speaking mix using descending then ascending glides. Ann Evans Watson describes a visual approach to achieving a bright belt quality and Billy Gollner takes us through a multi-step exercise to build chest-dominant sound for the high tenor. Beverly Patton describes four exercises aimed to stabilize the speech mix. A three-phase exercise contributed by Dr. Aaron Johnson uses a semi-occluded vocal tract to explore transition areas of the voice. He notes that the singer should "embrace the instability," with the ultimate goal being smoother transition from the low range to high. The "Honking" exercise described by Sarah Schneider initially uses exaggerated nasal resonance to help find a balanced chest mix. Dr. Kelly Holst's helpful meow mix encourages a vocal tract shape that facilitates forward, effortless

placement to establish mix with an enjoyable twist. Starr Cookman also created a three-part exercise to facilitate clear, stable phonation in the mix register. This exercise can be useful to facilitate balance phonation in this register that is neither pressed nor breathy. Lisa Popeil describes use of an /a/ slide to encourage the "laryngeal lean" in order to safely navigate higher pitch ranges in chest register. James Curtis and Brian Petty use a "hoot-n-holler" fun three-part exercise to coordinate easy, efficient voicing in chest, belting (high chest register), and head register. Finally, David Harris and Laurel Irene provide a playful exercise designed to explore CCM resonance strategies.

Chapter 8: Training Vocal Styles and Specialty Populations

The range of vocal styles required for the twenty-first-century hybrid singer is extensive. By no means are all CCM styles addressed within this chapter, but expert CCM teachers have contributed functional vocal technique exercises to explore many of the commonly found vocal styles, and in many cases the structure of the exercises can easily be modified for a variety of styles. Also included in this chapter are considerations for specialty populations including strategies for teachers required to train a CCM style within an ensemble and exercises for the older CCM singer. Audition preparation strategies for the vocal athlete are also included.

Dr. Norman Spivey has modified the traditional, bratty childhood taunting tune to access the belt-mix in higher ranges while maintaining articulatory accuracy and freedom. The forward placement of the consonant-vowel combination helps facilitate easy voicing while minimizing vocal effort. An important component to many CCM styles is maintenance of colloquial speech pronunciation without significant modification of vowels. Benjamin Czarnota developed an exercise to help the music theater singer navigate clear text in the higher belt range. Patricia Linhart uses "excited speech" as a basis for establishing high, forward placement for her belt/pop-style singing. Joan Ellison describes a belted "hey" exercise to introduce belting to singers who are new to that style. Jen DeRosa's four-part exercise also uses a speech-like quality to achieve a belt at higher pitches. Blissful belting, described by New York Broadway teacher Joan Lader, uses a bright vowel to facilitate appropriate placement and vocal tract configuration for pop/rock and music theater vocal styles. Chris York describes another creative four-part approach to belting. Matt Edwards created a fun exercise to facilitate tongue agility and help singers tune into the rhythmic beat associated with many CCM styles. Marcell Gauvin provides a jazz approach to song phrasing and Jeff Ramsey describes a multi-stem R&B riffing exercise. Dr. Wendy LeBorgne contributed a Multiple Personalities Vocal Exercise, combining posture, breath, phonation, and resonance strategies into one exercise for the CCM singer. Specifically designed for the singer learning to explore multiple vocal styles, this exercise provides an enjoyable approach to vocal play in a variety of singing styles. Also included in this chapter are two exercises addressing ensemble singing, as many CCM teachers are also involved in ensemble work. Edward Reisert and Tom Arduini have both contributed exercises emphasizing work to blend and balance a choral ensemble toward a CCM sound. Moving away from exercise addressing vocal technique, Sheri Sanders provides a unique acting exercise for use in preparing a pop/rock song. Naz Edwards takes us through a multi-step process to connect from story to song. We conclude this chapter with helpful audition tips by New York vocal coach Bob Marks on preparing a logical 16-bar cut for auditions.

5

Vocal Warm-Ups and Cool-Downs

The Motor Boat

Caroline Helton

Purpose of Exercise

■ To release the body of the tongue in coordination with sustained voiced sound
■ To relax the vocal tract while focusing sound forward

Origin of Exercise

We are all familiar with the benefits of tongue and lip trills as a vocal warm-up; these sustained voiced sounds require consistent, regulated airflow and work best when the vocal tract is relaxed, and the sound is directed toward the articulators involved. The "Motor Boat" works on the same principles, but requires and promotes a deeper level of relaxation of the tongue and jaw while generally using less airflow than it takes to sustain a tongue or lip trill.

Overview of Exercise

This low-intensity exercise serves as a precursor to entering the practice room and is easily done in conjunction with other activities of daily living (in the shower, making breakfast, etc.), so that the student can be well on her way to coordinated free vocalizing by the time she starts her practice session.

Exercise

1. Stick out the tip of the tongue and let the tongue lie over the bottom lip while the top lip stays in contact with the top of the tongue. Be very aware of the complete relaxation of the entire body of the tongue, as if it had received a shot of Novocain (Figure 5–1).
2. If you ever imitated a motorboat when you were a kid, this is probably how you did it: on a low pitch, use just enough sound to start the tongue vibrating against the bottom lip. (Tip: The more relaxed your tongue and jaw are, the better it works.) Make sure that the sound is voiced, or else it will sound more like a wet raspberry than a motorboat (Figure 5–2).
3. Some students can do it right away, and some need to work on it to get coordinated, so for those students you can start by having them try short motor boat trills ("blblblbl-ah/blblblbl-ah") beginning with the mouth open.
4. Once they get the hang of it, you can use the motor boat to siren through the range, taking note of where the tongue tends to grab and making sure to feel sensation and activity only where the tongue is vibrating against the bottom lip.

Figure 5–1. Relaxed tongue. Photograph courtesy of Caroline Helton.

Figure 5–2. Motor boat trills. Photograph courtesy of Caroline Helton.

5. You can then use this sound to transition into pitched vocalizing by singing scales or arpeggios beginning with the motor boat, but opening to an "ah" or an "uh" vowel.

Blowfish

Marci Daniels Rosenberg

Purpose of Exercise

- To create a sense of pharyngeal backpressure and resulting release
- To separate and differentiate tongue and jaw activity
- To promote efficient vocal fold vibration and forward placement
- To promote efficiently produced mixed registration

Origin of Exercise

This exercise was inspired by the work of Robert Sussuma, Guild Certified Feldenkrais™ Practitioner.

Overview of Exercise

The underlying principle of this exercise is that by executing this oral posture backpressure is generated in the pharynx resulting in a sense of increased space. This can be a useful kinesthetic experience particularly for students who have persistent constriction. The hierarchy of the exercise allows the voice user to generate this sense of space both with and without sound. Adding in the articulatory component promotes independence between the tongue and jaw while maintaining this space. This exercise can be completed on sustained sounds, with connected speech, and during singing. In contrast to many vocal exercises, the student will be generating a very **posterior** and **muffled** sound quality *during* this exercise but as a result, should appreciate a very noticeable calibration of voice with increased resonance and forward placement afterwards. The blowfish shape allows for connected speech and singing, making this is a very efficient vocal calibrator that can be used before more active voice use or singing, and throughout the day as needed. Additionally, this is a very useful tool to employ when singing in all styles. Creating an environment in which the tongue must function independently of the jaw can be very useful for helping to clarify vowels and improving resonance. In contemporary styles, this exercise is very effective at targeting mixed registration.

Exercise

The audio example is meant to demonstrate the muffled sound quality. They are just reference points. The blowfish configuration can be using with various speech and singing targets.

1. Sing or speak a simple phrase to establish a pre-exercise reference of sound and feel.
2. Exhale through very pursed lips with fully puffed cheeks (Figure 5–3).
3. Maintain a fully puffed posture during the controlled exhale through pursed lips.
4. Cue the student to notice a sense of stretch in the posterior pharynx and to observe a sense of expansion between the tonsils as if they were moving farther apart.
5. Repeat this a couple of times without sounds, noticing the change in space inside the throat.
6. Add a gentle sigh on the exhale in a comfortable speech range. This sound will be **very muffled** and posterior and not at all forward and buzzy as with many other exercises. This is OK. Maintaining the fully puffed cheeks throughout is important for achieving this posterior stretch and stretch muffled sound in the pharyngeal area. It also ensures that there is continuous, even airflow throughout the task. Repeat several times with various pitch contours in a comfortable range. If student struggles a bit with this simplify and allow them to explore and experience changes slowly. Sometimes this take some time.
7. Once the student can execute the above steps without cueing, have them articulate the sound /da/ in

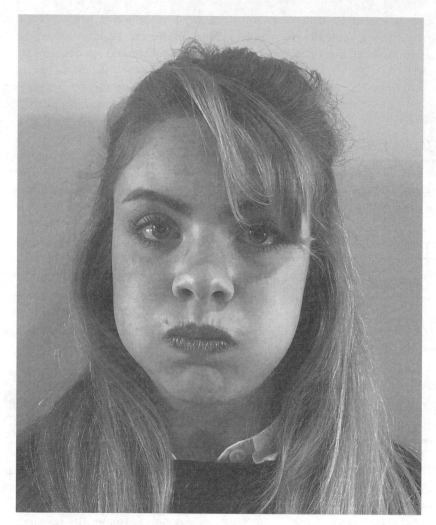

Figure 5–3. Blowfish exercise.

repetition within the blowfish shape. The goal here is to begin to differentiate the anterior tongue from the jaw function. Some may find this very difficult if their tongue and jaw are used to functioning in tandem. Allow time to differentiate the tongue and jaw movements as independent functions, as this is critical for full benefit. Don't rush the student.

8. Next differentiate the posterior aspect of the tongue /gagagagaga/. Once both anterior and posterior tongue can function independently from the jaw within the blowfish position, alternate between the two sounds, /digadigadigadigadig/. Combine anterior and posterior tongue with different vowels.

9. Once this is easy for the student, try other rote speech tasks such as months or days of the week. If the student has difficulty after several tries, return to a simpler version of the exercise. Proceed slowly but persistently, allowing the student to find the coordination in their own time. Don't skip through the spoken portion of these exercises, as it is important to move through all of the voicing "gears."

10. Repeat the /digadiga/ and other connected syllable combinations in singing. Scales and sung phrases can also be executed at this point.

11. In a normal manner, have the student repeat the initial phrase and notice differences.

Descending Five-Tone on Lip Trill

Norman Spivey

Purpose of Exercise

- To balance air and tone
- To simplify onset
- To find smoothness/legato between intervals

Origin of Exercise

Because onset can influence the vocalism throughout the phrase, I am interested in how the most balanced onset can be cultivated. This descending fifth exercise seems to be a way to find simple release of air and tone (lip trill), clean onset (vowel), and smooth legato.

Overview of Exercise

This is an exercise that I would recommend for all students (male and female, classical and musical theater). I typically use this exercise to begin warm-ups, and while it can be applied throughout the range, I tend to use it most in the middle voice. Later in a session I might take a phrase from a song and use these same techniques (lip trill and/or vowel) to address aspects of under- or over-energizing the tone, aspirated or glottal onset, or issues of legato. Although I tend to begin with the descending fifth, it can also be used effectively with other vocalizing patterns.

Exercise

I advocate beginning the lip trill unvoiced and then adding the voice to the flow of air. Students sometimes find an initial lack of coordination in adding their voice to the air, but it is almost always remedied with a few repetitions. This exercise helps develop an awareness of the roles of air and voice and ensures that the singer follows the age-old adage of "supporting the voice on the air." Once this has been established, transferring the exercise to a vowel is straightforward. A clean onset is expected, as is a smooth and vibrant flow from one pitch to the next—no bumps or glitches. Continue up and down by half-steps or other intervals.

Middle Voice Palate Stretch

Beverly A. Patton

Purpose of Exercise

- To stretch the soft palate by major thirds, perfect fifths, and octaves
- To increase range and stamina in the middle voice

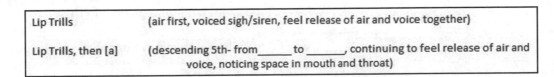

Origin of Exercise

I created this exercise in the studio.

Overview of Exercise

This exercise is appropriate for men and women and can be used in the middle of the warm-up for speech singing. "Oh" [o] offers the invitation to begin "calling" in the belt.

Part 1: "Oh No Ya Don't!"

Begin on C. On the phrase "Oh no ya don't," sing a major third, return to C and repeat the phrase using a perfect fifth, return to middle C and repeat the phrase again sliding up to an octave on "no," completing the phrase on the descending arpeggio. Go up by half steps then return on half-steps going up and down. Utilize a variety of actor "actions" such as scolding, cajoling, teasing, and so on.

Part 2: Belting/Calling on an Oh [o] Vowel, Octave Stretch

This is an extension from part I and works well for men and women in a group setting. Set a scenario, for example, a lawyer thinks he or she has solved the case. He or she points to others in the room and accuses them. Should be a dramatic and slightly "over the top" scenario to facilitate energized belt quality.

Mirening

Thomas Francis Burke III

Purpose of Exercise

■ To generalize the sense of vocal ease and most comfortable vocal effort found in semi-occluded vocal tract exercises to sung contexts
■ To establish a high tongue dorsum position for consistent brightness

Origin of Exercise

"Mirening" is derived from an Estill Voice Training exercise which integrates the concepts of "sirening" (glides on /ng/) for warm-ups and "mouthing the words."

Overview of Exercise

"Mirening" is an extension of a /ng/ glide exercise, "the Siren," used in Estill Voice Training (EVT). It can be used for warm-ups, cool-downs, marking or learning music, and problem solving certain "tricky spots." EVT uses the siren to increase range and establish most comfortable vocal effort and laryngeal positions for a given pitch or melody. Once students find ease on a single sound (i.e., /ng/), they are encouraged to generalize that sense of ease by "mouthing the words" of the song on pitch while retaining "the recipe" of the siren.

Exercise

1. Ensure optimal alignment.
2. Lengthen the cervical spine.
3. Slightly flare the nostrils and lift the ears without raising the eyebrows.
4. Release any extraneous tensions in the head, neck, or face.
5. Breathe silently through the mouth to establish an open throat position, or "false vocal fold" (FVF) retraction.
6. Produce the sound /ng/ as quietly as possible.
7. Ensure the tongue dorsum is in the high position against the top molars as in the word "sing" versus "sung."
8. Make light whimpering noises in the upper part of the range.
9. Glide down to the starting pitch of the song.
10. Sing the melody of the song maintaining the above recipe (flared nostrils, ears lifted, open throat/FVF retraction, whimpering).
11. Repeat, but this time mouth the words on pitch.
12. The tongue tip, lips, and jaw may move for articulation, but the tongue dorsum should remain high and velum low for the continued perception of the /ng/ in the sound.

Repeat the passage alternating between the "Miren" condition and "normal singing" as appropriate for the genre. Maintain the sense of ease and brightness in the sound with the tongue dorsum high.

The Gargle Exercise: Calibrate and Condition

Jennifer C. Muckala

Purpose of Exercise

- To condition the respiratory system and the phonatory system for rigorous use throughout the voice range
- To decondition recruitment of extraneous muscles of the larynx, tongue, and jaw during vocalization at all levels of rigor during lengthy use

Origin of Exercise

The only utilization of the gargle that I encountered in the early years of my career was introduced to me by Ed Stone, PhD. It was a method to facilitate voice in some of his most severe functional aphonic voice patients. I have found that it could be used as a more subtle tool in coaxing vocalization with a lower level of effort in rigorous voice use with singers. The broad majority of commercial voice users have had limited "formal" vocal training. Many of them will tell you that they have learned to "sing as they go"; the more unique the voice, the more highly it is often prized. Therefore, artists are often leery of vocal approaches that have a "formal" approach that might change a signature sound. The goals of the gargle are ease of production and consistency of function and access to the entire voice range at all dynamic levels. This exercise should help establish efficiency in the system. Stylistic choices in singing approach are largely untouched.

Overview of Exercise

Touring commercial artists are competing with as much as 120 dB of audience and concert noise during performances. Speaking and singing in loud, competing environments leads to habits of excessive recruitment of the strap muscles of the pressing, base of tongue tension, and jaw tension during heavy voice use. These habits are implicit in reports of vocal fatigue, reduced voice range, increased effort to produce voice, and deterioration in vocal quality. These complaints are well addressed with calibration exercises such as the gargle pre- and post-performance.

Water is a tool for monitoring the continuity of airflow and subglottic force during phonation. If the airflow is inconsistent, there is compensatory recruitment of muscle groups around the vocal folds to improve medial compression and maintain phonation; these ancillary muscles are rendered unnecessary when subglottic airflow is a constant. The bubbles are concrete evidence of the airflow consistency. Base of tongue tension release can be monitored acoustically during all levels of vocalization, from lower intensities to loud, prolonged voice use. The gargle is a simple enough task to allow the singer to attend to awareness of abdominal breath support, sensations of laryngeal effort during voice use, or resonation during functional use. Simplify the singer's focus to those targets: ease, efficiency, and access. When calibrated to a lower level of effort, the singer can then use it as a conditioning exercise to maintain greater ease of voice production at all vocal intensities. The idea is to establish a more physical connection to passive forces of respiration prior to recruiting active forces of respiration. It takes very little effort to release air in the lungs when they are at tidal capacity from the elastic recoil and Boyle's law. Once the singer has a confident grasp of the core exercise, a three-tiered warm-up and conditioning exercise may take 10 to 15 minutes as it prepares the voice for rigorous use throughout the voice range.

The Exercise Foundation

1. Take a small sip of water. Hold it in your mouth. A range of 1 to 3 cc (less than a teaspoon) is the most functional amount of water. Ideally, less is better. The liquid is purposed to create a seal over the airway to give the singer a concrete method to monitor airflow continuity during voicing attempts. As base of tongue tension reduces, less water will be more effective. For first-time attempts, ~4 cc (slightly less than a

teaspoon) may be necessary to facilitate confidence in airflow use and competence with this approach.

2. Take a breath through the nose, holding the water in the mouth. It is not necessary to breathe to tidal capacity (full lung) to perform this exercise. A comfortable breath to sustain the voice for 7 seconds is adequate in the beginning. The louder the vocal intensity and the longer you wish to sustain the voice, the more important it will become to breathe to tidal capacity.

3. Hold that breath and tip the head back—described as the image of a bobblehead—bobbing the head back on the atlas without collapsing the curvature of the neck or straining the front of the chin forward causing tension in the anterior muscles of the neck. An effective image for singers is to imagine they are looking at the top tier of an audience, to maintain proper alignment of the body and body mechanics during functional voice use.

4. Drop the jaw open to an "ah" position and lay your tongue forward—this direction is meant as a reference only. The target is a tongue that is neutral and disengaged in the mouth. Do not push the tongue forward, out of the mouth, or over the lower lip, as this will create a base of tongue engagement from overextension. This component is also a good "tell" on the singer who doesn't use continuous airflow during phonation. That individual will attempt to block the airway by pulling the tongue back to occlude the pharyngeal space, to prevent the liquid from being aspirated. Perceptually, this will sound like the centralized vowel "uh." The "ah" vowel is the target, as this acoustic output equates with the base of the tongue release and reduced pharyngeal constriction.

5. Direct the singer to release all the air in the lungs, as if the lungs were a deflating balloon. Initially, there may be the use of a more forceful exhalation as the singer begins and gains confidence in the approach. Acoustically, this has been described as a "motorboat" sound because anything that sounds like Morse code will make the singer choke!

6. Swallow the water before you start to run out of air!

Gargle Applications

1. Sustained single-tone production
2. Intervals of half step, whole step, thirds, fifths, and octaves

3. *Mezzo di voce* on single tone first, allowing the singer to increase vocal intensity with efficiency and a more calibrated approach to production

4. Use of gargle to sing through songs to establish ease at target intensities before taking the training wheels off

Straw Phonation to "Floaty" /u/ for Vocal Cool-Down

Kari Ragan

Purpose of Exercise

■ To assess perceived recovery level of the vocal folds after heavy singing load
■ To promote antagonistic muscle activity for vocal recovery for CCM singers performing predominantly in belt aesthetic
■ To initiate recovery of the voice to "neutral" after heavy singing load

Origin of Exercise

This exercise was originally designed for a subjective cool-down study (Ragan, 2013 and 2016). It was inspired by Ingo Titze's assertion that if soft and high voice is difficult, especially on the day after a strenuous vocal workout, the singer probably has not fully recovered. The fluid and structural protein disarray and repair occur mainly in the soft tissue directly under the skin of the vocal fold. It is the integrity of this tissue that is critical for soft voice at high pitches (Titze, 2009).

Overview of Exercise

Using this exercise as part of a cool-down protocol provides self-perceptual assessment during recovery after a heavy voice load and encourages the voice to return to "neutral." In particular for CCM singers using a predominantly belt aesthetic, singing an exercise that engages the antagonistic cricothyroid muscle after extensive thyroarytenoid muscle activity may be important to the cool-down process (see Chapter 1 in *The Vocal*

Athlete, Second Edition for further description of this). The benefits of Semi-Occluded Vocal Tract (SOVT) exercises, in particular straw phonation, have been largely substantiated by research. Straw phonation facilitates healthy vocal fold adduction due to the increased intraoral pressure in the vocal tract; it shapes and positions the vocal folds for efficient voicing. Using straw phonation at the onset of the exercise optimally sets up the singing voice before opening to the /u/ vowel. Sometimes an /u/ vowel, especially through the secondo passaggio or sung softly in a higher tessitura, can create tension due to potential laryngeal elevation for a singer unfamiliar with the exercise. To experience the benefit of this exercise, a singer must be carefully guided to functionally sing without such recruitment.

Exercise

1. Use the straw size and diameter of choice, noting that the narrower the straw, the higher the airflow resistance and intraoral pressure.
2. Straw phonate on the pitch B3 (men) and B4 (women), sustaining it for approximately 3 seconds. (The singer may choose a lower pitch if preferred; however, the aim of the exercise is to work through the secondo passaggio.)
3. Without stopping phonation, remove the straw and continue to sustain the same pitch, using a soft dynamic on a "floaty" /u/ vowel ("who").
4. Continue singing the soft, floaty /u/ on a five-note descending scale.
5. Repeat the same exercise ascending one half-step at a time to approximately F3 (men) or F4 (women). Cue the singer to be certain there is no laryngeal elevation or base-tongue recruitment when executing either the straw phonation or /u/ vowel portions of the exercise. The sound should be "turned over" and free from tension. Women should be in a light "head" registration and men will be in either a light "chest-mix" or light "head-mix" registration as the exercise ascends.

> If a student has considerable pharyngeal constriction, smaller diameter straw may be too challenging at first. Simply use a larger diameter and then explore from there

6. Continue the exercise, descending by half-steps, returning to the original starting pitch.

Note: A "floaty" /u/ vowel should be sung with a great deal of ease of vocal production and forward resonance, even at the soft dynamic level. No tension should be experienced.

Vocal Cool-Down Exercise for the Hybrid Singer

Renee O. Gottliebson

Purpose of Exercise

■ To initiate active recovery of the vocal mechanism after rigorous singing
■ To gently guide the voice to optimum pitch and resonance for speech

Origin of Exercise

The cool-down exercise presented for the hybrid singer is based on suggested practices in exercise physiology, vocal pedagogy, and professional voice care. Cooling down and stretching after strenuous exercise is commonly practiced among both elite and recreational athletes in order to reduce the risk of injury, prepare the large muscles for normal levels of activity, and improve overall fitness. These same principles may apply to the muscles of the vocal mechanism. Singers may benefit from gentle stretching and preparing the voice for healthy, resonant speech. The phrases selected for chanting and oral reading come from the protocol of Resonant Voice Therapy developed by Katherine Verdolini, which is based on the work by Arthur Lessac.

Overview of Exercise

The cool-down protocol for the hybrid singer begins by guiding the voice to optimum pitch levels for speech. A lip buzz is used to encourage breath support as well as reduced laryngeal tension. A descending loop is used to gently bring the voice to midrange pitches. The second exercise begins with deep breathing to induce relaxation, particularly of the chest, shoulders, and neck (increased tension in these areas has direct effects on the voice). Next, a yawn is produced in order to lower the larynx and to stretch and reduce tension in the oral and pharyngeal areas. The last exercise involves chanting and inflected oral reading of phrases at optimum pitch levels for speech. Nasal consonants are used to encourage forward placement of the voice. This activity serves as a reminder to continue to use good resonance for everyday speech.

Exercise

Part I: Tension Reduction and Pitch Finder for Speech

Inhale, allowing the abdomen to expand fully. Next, engage the abdominal muscles to support a lip buzz. Then using a lip buzz, begin at a comfortably high pitch and loop, descending a five-note scale. The loop involves a glide down of five notes and then back up a third, followed by another descent and up a third *again*, and so on to complete five connected loops (ending at a comfortably low pitch). The vocalizing should remain easy and focused. Repeat three times.

Part II: Stretching and Relaxation

1. Take a deep breath, inhaling slowly. Hold for a count of 3 seconds. Exhale slowly.

Repeat two times.

2. Take a deep breath, and upon inhalation, yawn, allowing the larynx to drop and the oral and pharyngeal spaces to truly open up and stretch. Repeat.

Part III: Resonant Speech

In order to engage good resonance for speech, chant the following on a comfortable, midrange pitch. Take a deep breath prior to each set, and take note of vibratory sensations in the front of the face (nasal passages and lips):

Set 1 "me" "may" "ma" "mo" "moo"

Set 2 "knee" "nay" "na" "no" "knew"

Repeat two times.

1. Chant the following phrases on a comfortable, midrange pitch. Second, read them aloud with normal inflection, maintaining a forward focus:
    1. Mary made me mad.
    2. Mother made marmalade.
    3. My mom may marry Marv.
    4. Marvin made mother merry.
    5. My merry mom made marmalade.
    6. No one knew Nanny.
    7. Nanny knew nothing.
    8. Now Nan knew Nelly.
    9. Nine knew nothing.
    10. Name nine new names now.

Lifting the Palate

J. Austin Collum, Emily Dunn, and Bari Hoffman Ruddy

Purpose of Exercises

- To elevate the soft palate throughout phonation and reduce excessive nasality
- To increase intraoral space for singing and lower the larynx
- To improve "warmth" of the singer's vocal timbre

Origin of Exercises

This exercise was first mentioned by Kristin Linklater in her first edition of *Freeing the Natural Voice* (Linklater, 1976). The exercise was designed to further actors' and singers' understanding of palatal lift. Linklater paired these strategies with a yawn-sigh technique to assist with maximal lift of the soft palate. As the performer yawned, he or she was instructed to "breathe in on the whispered /ka/." Following inhalation on a whispered /ka/, the performer then completed various vocalizes with consonant-vowel combinations (/haɪ-jaɪ-jaɪ-jaɪ/ or /haɪ-jə-jə-jə/) on one pitch, increasing by half steps over time. It was recommended by Linklater that the performer utilize a mirror throughout these exercises to observe the palatal lift throughout inhalation and phonation.

Overview of Exercises

While palatal lift is usually associated with a more classical style of singing, this exercise is beneficial for the CCM singer to bring awareness of the effects of palatal movement on nasality. This will allow the singer to feel an increased lift in the soft palate while simultaneously lowering the larynx. This exercise is especially beneficial for singers who want to explore a "warmer" sound and feel most comfortable in styles that use increased nasality.

Exercises

Exercise 1

The singer is to begin by producing a gentle /ka/ sound upon inhalation through the mouth. This can be paired with a yawn-sigh technique to assist with natural movement of the soft palate. The singer should feel a cooling sensation along the palate and the oropharynx, while the jaw naturally relaxes into an open posture. Thinking of the vowel shape /a/ while producing a gentle /k/ sound upon inhalation can assist with creating the optimal amount of intraoral space. If the palate is overly tensed or relaxed or if inhalation is too rapid, then a "snore-like" sound will occur. It is also important to note that no phonation should occur on inhalation. Once the singer feels comfortable with palatal lift, have the singer repeat the inhalatory /ka/ sound four or five times in a row in a staccato-like fashion to assist with an easy, natural lifting of the palate. Examples of these exercises are provided on the next page.

Exercise 2

Once a more natural sense of palatal lift has been achieved, it is time to begin initiating phonation while maintaining palatal lift. Have the singer begin with an easy /ka/ sound upon inhalation. Immediately following this inhalation, have the singer begin phonating on a descending five-note scale on /ja/. This can also be completed with ascending and/or descending fifths.

References

Guzman, M., Laukkanen, A., Krupa, P., et al. (2013). Vocal tract and glottal function during and after vocal exercising with resonance tube and straw. *Journal of Voice, 27*(4), 523.e.10.

Lessac, A. (1997). *The use and training of the human voice: A biodynamic approach to vocal life.* Mountain View, CA: Mayfield Publishing.

Linklater, K. (1976). *Freeing the natural voice.* Hollywood, CA: Drama.

Ragan, K. (2016). The impact of vocal cool-down exercises: A subjective study of singers' and listeners perceptions. *Journal of Voice, 30*(6), 764.e.1.

Ragan, K., Nevdahl, M., Eadie, T., & Merati, A. L. (2013). *The physiological and pedagogical basis for vocal cool-down exercises.* Presentation at the annual symposium "Care of the Professional Voice."

Titze, Ingo R. (2001). The five best vocal warm-up exercises. *Journal of Singing, 57*(3), 51.

Titze, Ingo R. (2002). How to use flow-resistant straws. *Journal of Singing, 58*(5), 429.

Titze, Ingo R. (2006). Voice training and therapy with a semi-occluded vocal tract: Rationale and scientific underpinnings. *Journal of Speech, Language, and Hearing Research, 49*(2), 448.

Titze, Ingo R. (2009). Unsolved mysteries about vocal fatigue and recovery. *Journal of Singing, 65*(4), 449.

Titze, Ingo R. (2018). Major benefits of semi-occluded vocal tract exercises. *Journal of Singing, 74*(3), 311.

Verdolini, K. (1998). Resonant voice therapy. In K. Verdolini (Ed.), *National Center for Voice and Speech's guide to vocology* (pp. 34–35). Iowa City, IA: National Center for Voice and Speech.

Notes

6

Laryngeal Strength and Coordination

Connecting the Voice to the Body and Breath

Stephanie Samaras

Purpose of Exercises

The purpose of this exercise in addition to a vocal warm-up is to facilitate understanding of how the sound is initiated from below (upper and lower abdominals controlling the exhale of breath).

Origin of Exercises

Exercise #1 (Yaw) is a Samaras original. Having to work with so many singers over the years, I had to devise an exaggerated way to get the first sound out without getting the voice off the breath, making it an extension of the intake. The second exercise: (a) "Hello," was introduced by one of my colleagues in NYC, although it was just sung on the same note. I added the octave to have the bottom and top notes in line with each other. (b) "Oh Yeah" I created as a reverse of "Hello" (top to bottom).

Overview of Exercises

Exercise #1

Get the student to relax jaw, drop it, and feel the throat relax as well on the intake. Feel the expansion below the rib cage and all the way around—like an inner tube. From that expansion (don't let go, stay expanded), say "Yaw" in your chest resonance-speaking voice on a pitch. Remember this is not singing! Feel the voice coming out from below the waist, no higher. One movement—jaw down, abdominals drop down at the same time. Use a low scoop to get the pitch level. This is extremely exaggerated—push down or out, if they keep collapsing before the pitch comes out. Keep at this a half-step at a time. You can also alternate "Yaw" with "Yeah" to keep the sound forward, not guttural. "Yeah" works well as the pitches get higher, and keeps it bright. This should not sound nasal. A fringe benefit from this is that it familiarizes the student with the belt voice, properly supported and placed well.

Exercise #2

a. "Hello." Go from chest resonance to head resonance, one octave. The singing should be very

97

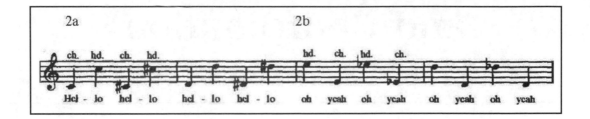

clearly placed in the front of the mouth, both the bottom and top notes. The jaw and support should drop down as you go up to the top note.

b. "Oh Yeah" is reversing the octave from top (head) to bottom (chest). Both pitches should be in line with each other, especially the bottom note.

Vocalise 1

Chest Voice (Male and Female)

Note. Teacher must use discretion as to how the high student can comfortably execute this. Try not to go any higher than C or C# above middle C at the first try. I have occasionally struck out with this exercise if students have trouble making a speaking tone on a pitch. (They want to "sing" on the given pitch.) If this is the case, I still continue with the exercise and allow them to "sing" the pitch. Although the exercise is not as effective, they still get good results.

Vocalise 2a and 2b

Remember to drop jaw and support down (working together) to go up in pitch.

Note. ch. indicates chest register, *hd.* indicates head register.

Clari-Bees

Katherine McConville

Purpose of Exercise

■ To maximize sound clarity and strength in those with healthy vocal fold edges
■ To recalibrate efficient use of airflow for singing

Origin of Exercise

This exercise is based on the theoretical underpinnings of Ingo Titze's research into the semi-occluded vocal tract (SOVT), which lead to an environment wherein the target sound can be altered somewhat to spare the vocal folds higher vibrational amplitudes and some of the vocal pitfalls that are associated with this. I tend to encourage many acutely injured singers with vocal fold lesions to back off their sound in favor of a higher airflow approach for a while, as healing progresses. However, I was finding that once these singers were returning to their normal repertoire, they were wasting air and sounding a bit breathy and cautious. I came up with this exercise as a way to return to a "core sound."

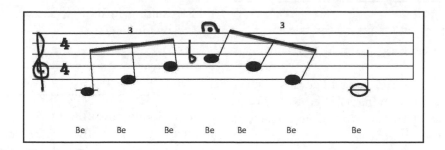

Overview of Exercise

This is a four- to six-sentence narrative of a general description of the exercise, including what vocal range is used for male or female (if applicable)—when it is appropriate to do (i.e., early in warm-up, after warm-up, cool-down, etc.); what scenarios might be appropriate for this exercise.

I prefer to do this exercise either later in a warm-up or after the warm-up, since the exercise might result in pressing if a singer hasn't gotten his or her breath support going. I find it most appropriate for singers (of any voice type) who are coming back from vocal injuries (namely lesions) and demonstrate a marked improvement in vocal fold edge appearance. I would use the exercise similarly in those with glottic insufficiency or weak, breathy sound.

Exercise

Start in the comfortable area of the middle range in chest voice (exercise may be extended into the mix if applicable). Lips should feel like they are being blown apart with loose cheeks at first and limited lip retraction. The rhythm of this exercise can be loose, and vowels can be sustained as desired to check for target clarity and comfort. As the singer begins to target a clearer or "pingy tone," lips are more firm on /b/ and wider mouth opening on the subsequent vowel is fine. If vocal fatigue or pressed vocal quality is noted, you can intersperse repetitions of the exercise with an /m/ (as in "me") with a focus on forward resonance and vibration, or simply scale the exercise back to mirror the earlier repetitions of "be" with loose lips and higher airflow.

Messa di Voce for Musical Theatre/Contemporary Commercial Music (CCM) Singers

Mary Saunders Barton

Purpose of Exercise

■ To promote laryngeal flexibility and to increase the singer's dynamic spectrum by coordinating treble and bass qualities in a flowing legato

Origin of Exercise

The exercise evolved out of my studio teaching process over a period of 20 years.

Overview of Exercise

This is a register balancing exercise. It is appropriate for men and women and can be taught to beginners-advanced singers and continued throughout their training. It is challenging because it creates instability in the voice. With patience, over time it can produce very satisfactory results.

The range of the exercise incorporates the primary register transition for women and the second register transition for men.

Eb 4–D5 for women

Eb 4–A5 for men

Exercise

Execute vowel sequence on a single pitch in a sustained legato.

Begin on "oo" in falsetto/head and gradually move to "oo" in speech (chest dominant), then to the open "ah" in a belt quality, then back to "oo" in speech resolving to "oo" in falsetto (head).

It helps to intone the exercise in speech to clarify the vocal qualities. The greater the contrasts (hooty, low laryngeal quality on the falsetto/head, twangy on the belt, and so on), the more useful this exercise will be.

Adding the consonant "y" in the first transition from head/falsetto to speech can help smooth the way. Oo . . . you . . . ah . . . you . . . oo

Cup Phonation: A Semi-occluded Vocal Tract Exercise

Marci Daniels Rosenberg

Purpose of Exercise

To relax vocal tract musculature and facilitate a favorable interaction between the vocal tract and the vocal folds resulting in more efficient vocal fold vibration and resonant voice.

Origin of Exercise

Semi-occluded vocal tract (SOVT) exercises are commonly used in voice training. The underlying principle of SOVT is that by introducing an occlusion somewhere above the level of the vocal folds, the level of vocal fold compression during phonation is to reduce because of the backpressure created at the occlusion. The occlusion redirects some of the acoustic pressure back down toward the vocal folds, resulting in a small amount of vocal fold abduction. This "unpresses" the vocal folds and facilitates more efficient vocal fold vibration. SOVT exercises come in many variations from most occlusive to least occlusive (Figure 6–1). The higher-resistance SOVTs are the most occlusive exercises (e.g., lip trill, stirring straws). These provide the most resistance and backpressure to "un-press" the vocal folds but are least likely connected to speech/singing. The least occlusive (i.e., closed, then open vowels) provide the least resistance but are most like connected speech/singing. Ultimately, it is beneficial to vary the level of resistance to maximize efficiency. The cup phonation exercise, unlike many variations of SOVT exercises (lip trills, hums, straw phonation,

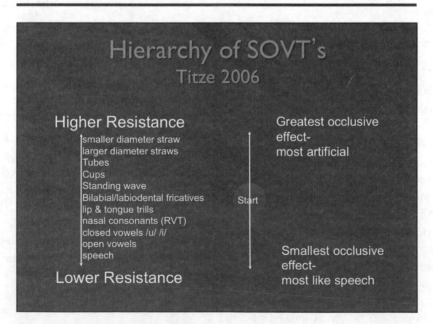

Figure 6–1. SOVT hierarchy.

hums), allows the singer to sing or speak different vowels and phrases while maintaining some level of occlusion (resistance). This technique can be very beneficial as part of a general voice warm-up routine or to work through problematic portions of a song. Additionally, it is a useful tool to facilitate a mixed registration and coordination of laryngeal adjustment to airflow.

Overview of Exercise

Singers can begin with higher-resistance SOVTs such as lip and tongue trills and hums. Straw phonation can then be introduced with wider-diameter straws (smoothie straws) to smaller-diameter straws (drinking straws). It is typically beneficial to practice many versions of SOVTs at different hierarchical levels and to vary them during practice in order to maximize motor learning of a SOVT during various vocal tasks. Singers should explore multiple dynamic and pitch ranges. Phrases of songs can also be sung using SOVTs such as singing the song through a straw first, then transferring to cup phonation described below.

Exercise

- Puncture a hole the diameter of a pencil into the bottom of a standard Styrofoam coffee cup (Figure 6–2A).
  - Different levels of resistance can be achieved by making the hole smaller or larger—gauge this based on the singer's response to the exercise.
  - Different levels of resistance can also be achieved by occluding the hole partially with the index finger.
- Place the wide, open portion of the cup around the mouth *completely sealing that area so that no air escapes around this part of the cup*, and

This exercise can be useful when working on developing a mixed register by gliding slowly 1-5-1 through the first transition area on /ae/ (hat) or /eh/ (hen) at moderate volume.

all air is directed out of the hole on the bottom (Figure 6–2B).
- Vocalize on a neutral vowel first, followed by a closed vowel /i/ in a comfortable range for several minutes.
- Vocalize in head register and chest register—1-3-1 and 1-5-1 glides work nicely.
- Introduce different vowels; /i/ works well as an initial vowel.
- Periodically revisit higher-resistance SOVT exercises (lip trill, straw) and vary the hierarchy.
- Sing or speak phrases using the cup—remember to maintain a complete seal.
- Repeat without the cup and note the difference in effort and placement in both speech and singing.

The Elusive Whistle Register: Hanging Out Up High

Jonelyn Langenstein and Brian E. Petty

Purpose of Exercise

- To build flexibility in the upper range
- To access the extreme upper range with ease

Origin of Exercise

Although not all singers require rehabilitation/habilitation with their extreme upper range, there are a few who have a real talent for singing up in the stratosphere (think Mariah Carey or Minnie Riperton). Using a SOVT, the singer can stretch the vocal folds to access these high notes without strain and better modulate the air pressure needed (or not needed) to live up in the rafters.

Overview of Exercise

This exercise will help all CCM singers to give the vocal folds a good stretch and build flexibility, although it is designed in particular for those who wish to access their very high "whistle register" and may need to do so

A

B

Figure 6–2. A. Preparing the cup. **B**. Position of cup.

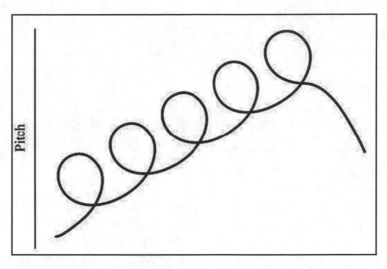

Figure 6–3. Ascending pitch.

with less tension and/or strain. This exercise is appropriate for both females and males, and it is important that the singer learn to monitor if and when tension or strain is felt. Before beginning, the singer should be fairly warmed up, especially in the mid- to upper range.

Exercise

On an /u/ vowel (as in "you"), the singer performs rollercoaster/siren pitch glides from midrange to mid-high range, then from high to mid-high range, then from high to higher range, and so on and so forth until the highest comfortable pitch is reached. The singer then glides back down to the midrange. One may find it helpful to keep the /u/ slightly nasalized throughout (Figure 6–3).

The exact pitches and number of ascending/descending glides are not important; the point is to keep tension out as higher and higher pitches are attempted. Ideally each siren series is performed in one breath at a comfortable to medium-soft volume. Abdominal breathing should be utilized, and it is important for the singer not to "overfill" the lungs as this can add unnecessary tension. Each time the pitch ascends, the abdomen should pulse inward slightly, coordinating abdominal breath support with the voice. This allows the singer to access higher notes without strain.

The breath does the work. The singer should not feel strain anywhere, and the tongue should be relaxed at the floor of the mouth. If the singer notices tension when approaching the higher range, pushing should be avoided. Instead, stop, take a breath, start on a pitch slightly lower than before, and complete the next ascending siren glide with ease. The singer should try to keep a slightly nasalized lip-rounded /u/ vowel. As the singer becomes more comfortable, hanging out up high without strain, a more open vowel can be attempted. The singer will then be able to maintain the higher range for longer periods of time and eventually access whistle register musical licks/riffs tension free.

Finding Efficient Vocal Fold Closure with Glottal Fry and Creaky Voice

Amelia A. Rollings

Purpose of Exercises

■ To feel the difference between pressed, balanced, and breathy vocal fold closure coordinations

- To be able to find and maintain a balanced vocal fold closure coordination throughout the range
- To encourage relaxation in the extrinsic laryngeal and facial musculature while simultaneously maintaining efficient vocal fold closure

Origin of Exercises

Every wind and brass instrumentalist understands the importance of practicing an embouchure that efficiently produces viable sound vibrations that can be amplified through the instrument's resonating chamber. Similar to an embouchure, a singer creates a source sound using vocal fold closure. A singer with a breathy vocal fold closure may demonstrate a weak tone with trouble negotiating long phrases and decreased stamina. Similarly, a singer with a pressed vocal fold closure may report feeling increased tension in the extrinsic musculature (e.g., tongue, jaw, forehead, sternocleidomastoid) and an increase in vocal fatigue or hoarseness after singing. Working on breathing or "relaxing" with these singers rarely works as it fails to remedy the primary problem occurring in the vocal fold closure rather than the symptoms he or she experiences. Glottal fry and creaky voice exercises have been used historically in both voice habilitation and rehabilitation. However, correct execution is essential, and the teacher must ensure that there is no strain or pressing when completing the exercise. For purposes of this exercise, students should be vocally healthy with no evidence of vocal fold lesions. If there is any question as to the status of the student's vocal health, these authors recommend not proceeding with this exercise.

Overview of Exercises

These exercises aim to more efficiently coordinate vocal fold closure in order for students to easily feel the small variances and the results they elicit. For the exercises below, "vocal fry" suggests a coordination lower than modal voice that has no perceptible pitch. "Creaky voice" strives to maintain the vocal fry coordination on given and perceptible pitches throughout the range.

The first exercise allows the singer to find, coordinate, and feel the gradations in vocal fold closure using vocal fry at no perceptible pitch. The second exercise

> If a student has a history of vocal fold lesions such as nodules, this glottal fry/creak exercise may not be indicated in a studio setting. Consider a semi-occluded vocal tract exercise such as straw phonation or cup phonation to facilitate efficient closure. As with all exercises, there should be no strain or discomfort.

asks singers to keep the balanced closure found in vocal fry as they transition to a modal pitch. And finally, in the third exercise, singers use creaky voice (a glottal fry coordination on a given and perceptible pitch) to more easily transition between the two vibrational modes. Glottal fry and creaky voice can be incorporated into a variety of teacher-designed exercises to help the vocally healthy singer find a more optimal vocal fold closure.

Exercises

Exercise 1: Closure Gradations

1. Find a relaxed glottal fry on the [a] vowel. (If students cannot find a relaxed glottal fry immediately, have them call or moan [na] and fall in pitch until they reach a fry coordination. The resulting fry should be a low, imperceptible pitch, resembling a cat purr. All external laryngeal musculature, tongue, facial posture, etc., should be completely relaxed. Encourage the student to notice this feeling of relaxation while maintaining efficient vocal fold closure.) It is very important to monitor that there is no sense of strain of effort in the throat when completing this exercise.
2. Alternate between glottal fry and breathy closure coordinations.
3. Alternate between glottal fry and *slightly* pressed closure coordinations. (The student will notice that the pitch will raise when performing the slightly pressed closure coordination.)
4. Perform the full vocal fold closure gradation exercise while noticing the small nuanced gradations between coordinations:

   Fry – Breathy – Fry – Pressed – Fry – Breathy – Fry – Pressed – Fry

Exercise 2: *Fry to Pitch*

1. Find a relaxed glottal fry on the [a] vowel or [i] vowel. (For males and females in a classical/operatic style, start with the [a] vowel E4 and lower and the [i] vowel F4 and higher; adjust vowel choice as needed based on acoustic adjustments needed for vocal style and range.)

2. Slide to the upper pitch and sing the pattern 5-4-3-2-1 while keeping the closure coordination balanced and external musculature relaxed. (If the closure becomes breathy or pressed when sliding from fry to the pitch in modal voice, have students exaggerate the problem, feel the difference, and repeat while keeping a more balanced closure [neither breathy or pressed].)

Exercise 3: *Creaky Voice*

1. Find a creaky voice coordination (aiming to produce a glottal fry coordination on the highest pitch of the scale) on the [a] vowel or [i] vowel on the top pitch of a five-tone scale (5-4-3-2-1). (For males and females in a classical/operatic style, start with the [a] vowel E4 and lower and the [i] vowel F4 and higher; adjust vowel choice as needed based on acoustic adjustments needed for vocal style and range.)

2. While keeping the balanced closure found with the creaky voice, transition to a full voice (modal) coordination and slide down the scale from 5-4-3-2-1.

Notes

7

Registration and Vocal Tract Modification

Head Voice Stability

Sarah Maines

Purpose of Exercise

- To develop the ability to remain in light, forward head voice registration during ascending patterns throughout the middle and high range
- To optimally balance respiration, phonation, and resonance during high onsets and quick, light, legit patterns
- To practice modifying a legit, rounded /u/ vowel above the staff for female singers
- To expand the upper female range

Origin of Exercise

This exercise comes from Janette Ogg, DMA, Professor Emerita, Shenandoah Conservatory. Dr. Ogg taught it to me as a classical exercise, intended to encourage lightness, freedom from tension, and flexibility in the voice throughout the range. I have used the exercise with many singers but find it particularly helpful with adolescent girls who are strong belters and weak legit singers. When singing an ascending pattern

in a legit song, these girls often carry too much chest voice up from the lower pitches. The frequent octave leaps and ascending arpeggio patterns in "Think of Me" may serve as prime musical examples of this vocal behavior. This may be a result of inexperience, a thyroarytenoid versus cricothryoid muscle imbalance, little coordination between the three subsystems of voice, or a combination of many of these factors. The exercise can also be helpful for teens who wish to riff in their head voice but lack control or flexibility. As the exercise begins with a descending pattern before rapidly ascending, the singer can learn to maintain the sense of lightness from the onset throughout the entire phrase. Principles of lowered subglottic pressure and glottal resistance for legit singing versus belting are evident in this exercise, in addition to principles of legit vowel modification above the second female passaggio.

Overview of Exercise

The singer will begin by establishing a round, forward, hootie sound on /hu/. The singer will then apply that vowel to a rapid triplet arpeggio pattern in the mid voice, striving for forward resonance, lightness, and freedom. Once the midrange is solid, the singer will gradually take the exercise as high as she/he/they can comfortably go while maintaining forward resonance

107

and freedom from tension. Vowel modification will be necessary for the upper pitches.

Exercise

Step 1

Hoot like an owl, in head voice on the vowel /hu/, on any comfortably high pitch. The vowel should be tall and rounded, and the tongue should be forward and relaxed inside the mouth. Be sure to breathe through the shape of this vowel. There should be a pleasant sense of resonant energy forward in the face when hooting. This often feels like a slight buzzing or vibration on the roof of the mouth or behind the nose. Many singers trying this for the first time describe the feeling as "hollow," with an awareness of a high volume of air gushing through their mouth and throat.

Step 2

When the hooting feels very comfortable, sing the notated pattern on that same vowel. Move up by semitones in the most comfortable part of your midrange. Strive to keep the same vowel and pleasant sense of resonant energy forward in the face throughout the whole exercise. Pay particular attention to the second treble C in the exercise. Does it feel the same as the onset of the exercise?

Step 3

Take the exercise as high as you can without adding tension. Be sure to drop the jaw and modify the vowel of the highest pitches to /o/ around Eb5, /a/ around F#5, and /ae/ around C6 as you ascend. The sound should remain small, light, resonant, and easy throughout the exercise.

You Send Me

Kathryn Green

Purpose of Exercise

- To extend the upper range of the male head voice
- To balance registration as the voice moves from head to head-dominant mix and to chest-dominant mix
- To develop "riffing" abilities by encouraging the student to ornament the melodic line

Origin of Exercise

Many of my musical theatre students are asked to prepare pop songs from the 1950s and 1960s for their audition packets. Right about the time the successful Broadway musical *Jersey Boys* opened, I came up with the idea of applying the falsetto quality used in that show as a way to encourage young male voice students to practice in their head/falsetto voice. This particular exercise also lends itself to easy experimentation with stylized "riffing" or embellishments of the melodic line. The goal is to produce a viable sound with minimum stress to the vocal mechanism and to develop flexibility.

Overview of Exercise

This exercise starts with an [u] vowel that descends down to the last two notes on an open and closed E vowel. This vowel progression causes typical students to stay in a head-dominant registration until they arrive at the last two notes when the vowel changes. It is relatively easy for the student to segue to the mixed

You_____ send me_____ Dar lin' You_____ send me

chest register from the falsetto quality at that point. It is appropriate to use early in the lesson, either shortly after warming up the chest register or as the first exercise of the day, particularly if the student has difficulty pulling up too much chest in the upper range. This exercise is best initiated in the head register of the male singer using the falsetto quality. The advantage of this approach versus traditional vocalizing is in student compliance. Because this exercise is derived from an actual song, students are more likely to use it in practice than an exercise composed of vowels and a stepwise musical pattern.

Exercise: Step-by-Step Instruction on How to Complete the Exercise

- Begin the exercise substantially above the male passaggio (D4–F4) in the head voice with falsetto quality; C5 is often a good starting point.
- After students are comfortable with the melodic line, encourage them to start adding stylized ornamentation or their own embellishments to the line.
- The tempo needs to be slow enough for the student to be able to take the time to find the embellishments and experiment.
- Repeat the phrase, descending by half-steps until the student reaches the point where the voice is comfortably transitioning into chest-dominant mix.
- Instruct students to allow their larynx to rise and fall as needed.
- Once the phrase has been taken all the way down, start taking it back up by half-steps. Encourage the student to allow the voice to reintroduce the

lighter quality without abruptly shifting over to a pure falsetto.

Pinball Wizard

Kathryn Green

Purpose of Exercise

- To warm up and strengthen the muscles of the falsetto register
- To balance registration as the voice moves from falsetto to chest and back
- To encourage young singers to explore the upper head/falsetto register

Origin of Exercise

Young male singers are generally not comfortable exploring the falsetto register as it usually sounds and feels too disconnected and effeminate. A few years ago while working with singers in a production of *Tommy*, the musical based on the music of the rock group The Who, I found that the stratospheric range required in the leading male roles was both a challenge and a great opportunity to introduce young male singers to the use of the falsetto register. This exercise isolates one of the most difficult phrases of "The Pinball Wizard" as a vocalize and has been designed to develop the ability to sing in an extended rock tenor range by negotiating the registration in combination with

Pinball Wizard Exercise

Sure   plays   a   mean   pin - ball____

resonance strategies. The goal is to produce a viable rock belt sound with a minimum of strain and trauma to the vocal instrument.

Overview of Exercise

This exercise is best initiated in the falsetto register of the male singer. It is appropriate to use early in the lesson, either shortly after warming up the chest register or as the first exercise of the day, particularly if the student has difficulty pulling up too much chest in the higher ranges. It is useful for both the tenor and baritone singer, although the tenor voice will generally be able to negotiate a mix more readily than the baritone. The students were very enthusiastic about exploring the falsetto register with this particular exercise, as they perceived the sound to be closely related to that of male-dominated rock singing as opposed to an ethereal exercise not related to their vocal goals and objectives.

Exercise

■ The exercise should be started substantially above the male passaggio (D4–F4) in the falsetto voice around C5.
■ The words may be used initially, but if students exhibit any difficulty with the execution of the words, ask them to sing the whole phrase on an [ae] vowel with a lateral "smile" position of the mouth.
■ Tempo is not important; let students establish the speed at which they sing the descending phrase.
■ Repeat the phrase, descending each time by one half-step until the phrase reaches the point where the voice more easily sings in the chest register throughout the phrase.
■ As students sing each lowered phrase, encourage them to allow the voice to migrate to whatever mixed registration is possible.
■ Once the phrase has been taken all the way down, start taking it back up by a half-step, again encouraging the student to allow the voice to reintroduce the lighter quality without abruptly shifting over to a pure falsetto registration from the chest-dominant tone.

Released Vocal Regulation

Martin L. Spencer

Purpose of Exercise

■ To regulate airflow, resonance, and phonation
■ To promote smooth passaggio transition

Origin of Exercise

The most common pathologies encountered in contemporary commercial music (CCM) students and performers may be secondary to an overly chest-dominant "mix." This is a desirable phonation mode for midrange and upper midrange belt quality, but may induce phonotrauma if not calibrated for consistent ease. Forcing of an uncalibrated chest register up through the passaggio promotes "slapping" vocal fold closure patterns. Across time, this may lead to transient, medial, midthird true vocal fold (TVF) swelling. If continued, this aggressive closure pattern may degrade swelling to more concerning nontransient thickening of the vocal folds, chronic inflammation, and eventually fibrous lesions (e.g., "nodules"). A singer should realize that progressive loss of mid and high-range ease, loss of dynamic flexibility, and richer low range may be pathologic symptoms.

Singing rehabilitation may focus on reduced passaggio pressures to encourage a medial "lapping," rather than "slapping," of the folds. A key to eased regulation may be found in this exercise that facilitates sliding pitch movement through low chest register into the "mix," curving into high head register, and then sliding back down through low chest . . . all across the span of one breath (e.g., a rising and falling pitch glide). As a voice pathologist, I find it very interesting to note how little range and dynamic consistency is typically demonstrated during initial patient iterations of this exercise. Often, a singer will crescendo with rising pitch to force the voice into an uncontrolled forte or fortissimo in the "money" range of high belt. Additionally, many singers demonstrate poor awareness of usable upper and lower pitch maxima. It is hoped that this exercise will concentrate focus on "released vocal regulation," thereby promoting consistency across busy academic schedules, intensive professional rehearsal periods, and ultimately, successful eight-show weeks.

Overview of Exercise

A low range, sliding, aspirated onset is facilitated by chest-centered resonance and airflow rising through the thorax. Singers may undesirably grab the lowest pitches, producing a suddenly tensed tone, which typically intensifies with further pitch elevation. The image of a violin bow already moving before it starts to caress the string is a helpful image to facilitate reduced vocal grabbing. Hums, or a sustained /u/, ease passaggio transition through increased vocal tract inertance and compliance (a discussion of vocal tract inertance and compliance is found in Chapter 16 in the companion textbook *The Vocal Athlete, Second Edition*). Provide an initial model of optimal range traversal for your singer. As a teacher or clinician, your model should be free of tensions such as unintended facial grimaces, neck contractions, or averted gaze; your singer will be encouraged to mirror your simplicity. It is typical for singers to have a poor expectation of mid-high to high pitch range production, and they will plateau or change pitch direction too early for their innate ability. Circles of progressively ascending movement, starting in high midrange or low high range, may aid a singer in realizing their true upper pitch limit (Figure 7–1). Encourage an alternative cognitive focus, from "How do I sound?" to "How does resonant perception progressively narrow and elevate through the mask?" Changing the vowel to /i/ and /ae/ helps to keep laryngeal

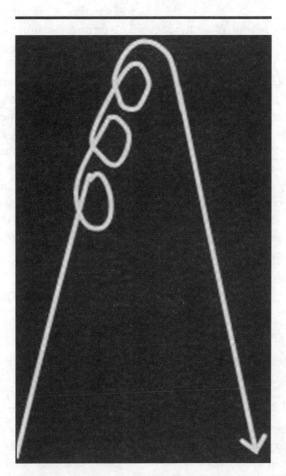

Figure 7–1. Circles of progressively ascending movement.

positioning relatively raised and brightens the tone for a twangy belt aesthetic. (Note that /u/ may be more helpful in a voice rehabilitation scenario to promote a more classical resonance.)

Exercise

Part I: Released Pitch Glides

Place your fingertips lightly on the bridge of your nose. Allow your thumb tips to rest on the lower jaw. Comfortably inflate with air and sigh across a low-pitched vocal onset. Rise in pitch and focus on sympathetic, resonant elevation. Glide over a comfortably high pitch maximum, and then descend through low pitch range to an aspirate tonal release. If your voice is not warmed up, try several exercise iterations to bloom through your passaggio. There is nothing wrong with the occasional mid-high or high range "hesitation"; you're warming up and not performing! The pedagogue should note smooth passaggio transition and even dynamic control. Ultimately, exercise performance should be consistent in range across iterations.

Part II: Cross-Passaggio Octave Portamenti

The combination of differential thyroarytenoid cricothyroid activation in tandem with smoothed mucosal movement of the vocal fold through the mix may better be applied to singing technique with the introduction of "marker" pitches, one octave apart, which encompass the zona di passaggio. For example, if a female's primary register transition is in the zone from F4 to Bb4, then boundary marker pitches may be chosen from D4 to D5. The starting tone (D4) should be sustained as under a fermata on a bright vowel. This marker should be characterized by even tone, sufficient body resonance,

vibrato (if typically present), and singing quality intensity at a supported mezzo piano (or better yet specification of the theoretical mezzo that lies between mp and mf). Do not continue the exercise if the initial marker tone is not sustained for several seconds with these characteristics. Once successfully sustained, the singer will slowly and smoothly portamento to a sustained higher octave. Typically when learning this exercise, the singer will sustain the lower octave too long and then make an abrupt transition to the higher pitch. This tendency must be addressed by the clinician/pedagogue, so that a slower controlled release to the higher pitch is facilitated. Hand movements and duetting are handy facilitating devices. Careful monitoring and dissipation of secondary tensions will yield optimal technical outcome. Once an initial octave is stabilized, then the series may be transposed up or down by semitones to further tailor need to patient ability. (As a tenor, I perform this exercise from G3 to G4 as part of my daily practice.) A final transition to melody is accomplished by inserting a major scale into the octave and using continued, careful monitoring of tension and dynamic through the releasing mix.

Swing Arpeggio

Michelle Rosen

Purpose of Exercise

The purpose of the exercise is to elicit an easy, light, unpressured chest mix and take it up over the traditional break. I usc this exercise toward the end of the technique portion of a lesson, after having isolated (and strengthened) chest and head registers.

Origin of Exercise

The exercise is based upon arpeggios we all do, but differs in two important ways: melodically it deviates from the ubiquity of the major arpeggio (1358531) and rhythmically it is syncopated. Those two alterations plus the incorporation of colloquial speech allow for a smoother, more appropriate segue into jazz, pop, or musical theatre repertoire. It bridges the gap between vocalise and repertoire.

Exercise

Starting pitch for women can be approximately A3, for men approximately C3. The pitches are an arpeggiated major 7 chord (1357531), syncopated as shown. Text can vary, but I usually start with "I'm gonna have a good time" so that the /ae/ vowel, which lends itself to a mixy quality, is on the 7. Volume should start at no louder than moderate. The repetitions go up by half-steps and then back down. After a few minutes, I vary the text so that other vowels are on the highest pitch, such as "I want to buy a new dress," "It is a very nice day," and "I want to wear my new shoes." Once the student has successfully maintained the mix throughout a range of pitches, I will ask for different intensities (louder, softer) to see if that affects the ability to keep the light mix going.

Speech-like Arpeggios

Norman Spivey

Purpose of Exercise

- To find a speech-like production on pitch
- To translate speech to a sung tone

- To increase the range (high and low) of available speech-like singing
- To find an easy, open speech/belt quality

Origin of Exercise

An exercise that mirrors speech patterns can be helpful to singers in learning to make the transition from speech to song and in developing the importance of intention in the sung monologue. This exercise takes a traditional arpeggio and combines it with a simple text (the text can be modified to include other vowels and/or sentiments).

Overview of Exercise

Any exercise that works with speech to singing naturally presupposes a healthy, vibrant speaking voice. If this is not the case, some remedial speech work may be needed. I have found this exercise to be effective with both male and female students in exploring a more speech-like approach to the singing voice. To begin, I like to find a place in the range where the voice can be comfortable—maybe around C4 or D4 for men and around G5 for women. Then we work through the range—up the scale, going toward a "call" or a "belt," and down toward the bottom of the range to work on the clarity of speech and tone in that area. I find it to be a useful addition to a warm-up.

Exercise

I typically begin this exercise by speaking the word "Hi!" on an elevated pitch and having the student repeat the text on the same pitch. Then the spoken word is placed on the pitches of the arpeggio. Singers new to this may revert to a more "sung" tone initially than

the spoken "Hi!," but with repetition and encouragement, they can easily replicate their speech feel on the notes of the scale.

Sustained (2nd, 3rd, 5th, and Octave) Glide

Bari Hoffman Ruddy and Adam Lloyd

Purpose of Exercise

- To improve breath coordination and vocal endurance
- To blend registers and reduce voice breaks
- To expand vocal range

Origin of Exercise

Contemporary and commercial musicians may not utilize vocal exercises during their daily performing and singing activities. These performers sometimes push the limits belting loud and high, screaming, flipping between chest and head voice . . . and so forth. These performers sometimes complain of developing "holes" in their voice and "voice breaks" between registers. This exercise is physiologically based, with some principles of the Stemple Vocal Function Exercises (Stemple, Lee, D'Amico, & Pickup, 1994) and Titze's Semi-occluded Vocal Tract Exercises (Titze, 2006) influencing its development.

Overview of Exercise

This exercise seeks to balance respiration, phonation, and resonance by using slow gliding intervals. It is progressive in range and duration. The intended outcome of this exercise is to improve breath coordination, balancing intrinsic laryngeal muscle function and decreasing voice breaks and shifts in registers. The singer is asked to take a comfortable breathing and slow glide from a comfortably low pitch up a whole step and then back down, increasing the interval to a 3rd, 5th, and then an octave as able. The exercise should be produced with a softly engaged voice.

Exercise

This exercise should be performed through one's comfortable range. Start on a comfortably low pitch (perhaps C3 for men and C4 for women). Range will vary with voice type. Begin by taking a comfortably deep inhalation. With an easy onset, sustain the first pitch on the sound /no/, or a lip buzz, a tongue trill, or a raspberry. Next, begin to glide up to a whole step above and slowly back down to the beginning pitch. Slow the tempo and duration of the exercise as able to improve breath coordination. Increase the range of the exercise to a 3rd, 5th, and an octave as comfortable. This exercise should be performed with a softly

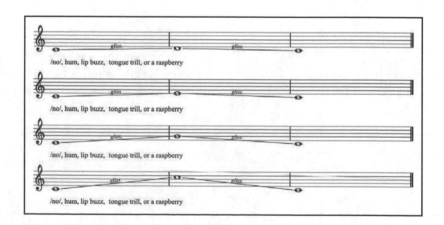

engaged voice, carefully maintaining a steady flow of exhaled air, a relaxed sensation in the throat, and noticing a consistent vibrational sensation in the mouth and on the lips. This exercise can be completed in chest voice, head voice, as well as mixed voice.

> A "baritenor" is a singer who is more naturally a baritone with a tenor extension. This is more commonly seen in the musical theatre genre.

Accessing "Mix"

Jeannette L. LoVetri

Purpose of Exercise

To isolate, cultivate, and strengthen a "mix" of the vocal registers called "chest" and "head" or modal and loft or TA and CT dominant, particularly across mid-range pitches.

■ Allow the "speaking quality" to ascend in pitch without excess strain on the vocal folds or tension in the neck muscles.
■ Allow the singer to use "colloquial pronunciation," avoiding modification of vowels for resonance or aesthetic purposes
■ To help maintain expressive authenticity by maintaining a more direct connection to speech-based sounds

Origin of Exercise

This exercise came from my own experience as a singer who was trained to sing in a "natural manner" without any focus upon vocal registers, my exposure to the New York City Broadway community, and through my 45 years work with professional singers of CCM styles. The strongest influence on the exercise was the work of Cornelius Reid, which was aimed at classical singers but which I modified to be useful to other kinds of vocalists.

Overview of Exercise

This exercise is to help blend the vocal registers across the mid-pitch range of both men and women. In higher voiced women and men (sopranos and tenors) the middle pitch range is across approximately G/A above middle C or G4 and A5. In lower voices (baritones and "baritenors," mezzos and contraltos) approximately E/F/G above middle C or E4, F4, and G4. Low basses generally do not sing in this "mix" quality but it can sometimes be found in lower voiced men who can sing in a lighter quality (softer and less deliberately resonant in a classical manner). In children who sing music theater it is useful as an alternative to a full belt or singing in an "angelic" head register sound.

When to Do This Exercise

This exercise should be done after the voice is completely warmed up and comfortable, using whatever exercises accomplish that task. It presupposes, however, that the vocalist has at his or her disposal two independent, strong, and comfortable registers called "chest" and "head" to use.

It is important that deliberate use of "register quality" is not the same as being able to sustain a low-pitched sound or a high-pitched one. The quality of each register should be robust in and of itself. The chest, or lower, register in both men and women should be loud *without force*, rich in tone and acoustic harmonics and solid or firm. In women, when developed, it covers anything from E3 or F3 below middle C up to G3 or A4, or, in a CCM singer, up to as far as C5. The head register, in its purest sense, is clear and often described as being "silvery." It can become quite loud (mimicking the sound of a classical counter tenor). When both of these registers can be easily sung across the mid-range pitches at about mezzo forte, the tendency of the sound would be to carry aspects of both registers at the same time. In traditional classical pedagogy, it is often referred to as being "chiaroscuro" or light and dark simultaneously. This word often describes the balance of light and dark in fine art as well.

When both registers are independently available, it should be possible to sing the mid-range pitches in either "chest" or "head" dominant quality according to the singer's choice.

One way to determine if the mid-range pitches are balanced is to examine the vowel sounds scrupulously. They should remain consistent, unchanged from low to high except where the vowel is deliberately modified for artistic purposes. It should be easy to adjust the volume without disturbing either the vowel or the vocal quality. The difficulty of the exercise is to achieve this equilibrium, but when done correctly, slowly and with care, it liberates both the voice and the artist to be as expressive as possible. Provided the throat is not manipulated directly in any way, the freedom afforded by this exercise cannot be replaced by any other vocal behavior.

"Mix," therefore, implies that there is a balance of vocal fold response (open/closed quotient), breath pressure (graduated increase or decrease as needed), and resonance adjustment (vowel sound configuration in the vocal tract) and that this "mix," when properly executed, can be used easily with consonants, in a range of volumes and in repertoire.

Exercise

The head of the vocalist is centered over the neck, which is released. The body is erect, and the singer should keep the inhalation low into the torso, allowing the abdomen to expand on inhalation. The body must maintain an open and stable rib cage and deliberate and controlled use of the abdominal muscles during phonation, gradually lifting and tightening them during singing. Initially, the head should be slightly tilted up (about 45%) without stress to the cervical spine, and the face should be in a broad, wide, but comfortable smile, with the jaw dropped a *moderate* amount and the lips retracted towards the earlobes, in a smile. The tongue should be forward, flat in front and relaxed inside the mouth, with the tip resting lightly over the bottom teeth on the lower lip. The tongue should not flatten out or be allowed to drop back into the throat. The face should be animated and the singer should think of or visualize the muscles of the soft palate as being raised as they would be just before a sneeze or a laugh. *That this set up is done correctly, with atten-tion to detail, is crucial.* Wrong configurations here will prevent the exercise from doing its job.

The singer should sing /ae/ as in hat as found in Standard American English, on a low pitch (such as G3) and smoothly slide (glissando) up an octave, maintaining the vowel sound, keeping the face, head, and jaw opening steady and the volume moderate while singing. The vowel on the high pitch should match in quality to the one on the lower pitch. *The throat should feel unpressured and free.* The breath should be steady, with neither extreme tension in the abdominals nor laxity. The vocalist should proceed by half steps on the same exercise, until they reach above the mid-pitch range (typically called the passaggio or "the break). Then the singer should go down by half steps to the starting note. The quality of the tone should be "bright" and "speaky" but also warm and open. It is not necessary to focus any awareness on a special kind of "resonance" but rather on pitch, intensity (volume), and freedom of execution while keeping the vowel undistorted. When this is over, the singer may proceed to re-position the head to a more normal position and to change to other vowels such as /i/, with the same musical pattern and function goal: comfort and freedom.

The execution of this or any other vocal exercise has to do with a number of factors that must be properly coordinated and done simultaneously or they will not be effective. Only someone with a strong knowledge of the mix quality as found in repertoire should evaluate its execution. It does not sound like "classical" vocal production when done correctly and should not be compared to that quality functionally. Mix allows the vocalist to sing in a quality that most experts would call "chest" but in an easier, lighter vocal production that allows the vocal folds to do less work while allowing the tongue to remain flexible enough to change position without struggle and to sing in a brighter, louder, more spoken quality in "head," ascending to the highest pitches as needed.

Some vocalists sing in one register. Ethel Merman was known for saying there was just one. Some classical singers, especially females, strive to keep the low pitches as light as possible in order to avoid an obvious "break" or abrupt auditory shift. Some singers use only mix, keeping their sound light but energized enough to be heard. They are often jazz vocalists who rely on electronic amplification. There is no harm to the voice

in this production but it will limit the "colors" or timbral quality of the singing, as well as the volume or intensity and the range, making both more limited.

Vocalizing the Speaking Mix

Mary Saunders Barton

Purpose of Exercise

- To develop coordination in the middle voice between head and speech functions

Origin of Exercise

My recollection is that I began to absorb some of these middle voice exercises in the 1980s through my contact with Joan Lader (via Jo Estill) and Marianne Challis. The obvious extension seemed to be to coordinate the mixed middle with head voice in a seamless continuum.

Overview of Exercise

The exercise is great for young women trying to build a connection between their middle and top voices. It encourages delaying the second passaggio to E flat 5. The optimum range for the exercise is to top out around G5.

Exercise

Execute the descending thirds in a clear speech mix and then slide up the octave into a floated head quality. Make a strong contrast in functions. Exercise should

feel buoyant, not effortful, although it is critical to hang on to the speech quality in the descending sequences.

Four Exercises for Simple Speech

Beverly A. Patton

Purpose of Exercises

Speech mix in musical theatre is a key component. These exercises are designed to:

- explore more closed speech-like vowels
- maintain open soft palate
- encourage an acting component

Origin of Exercises

Trial and error has given me the opportunity to find easy sentences that retain a variety of open and closed vowels in a way that is easy to remember and reproduce.

Overview of Exercises

These exercises are for use early in the lesson for speech clarity and to increase range. Find appropriate keys for men and women. It is imperative that each exercise has a "point of view" from the singer so that specific actions can be employed, such as sarcasm, anger, seduction, and so on. Use this early in the warm-up of the middle voice. Exercise #3 introduces "The Mother Vowel of the Middle Voice" for musical theatre, the remarkable "eh." Exercise #4 uses the "f" to create an easy flow of air.

Exercise #1

Five-note descending scale, beginning on G and then going up chromatically by half-steps.

"Say it isn't so!"

Exercise #2

Pitches 551 going up and down the chromatic scale.

"He said no!" (alternate with "She said no!" "They said no!" "I said no!")

Exercise #3

Pitches 8531 then reverse 1358 "Yeahyeahyeahyeah"

Exercise #4

Pitches 8531 then reverse 1358 "FeeFiFoFum"

Register Transition Exploration

Aaron M. Johnson

Purpose of Exercise

■ To explore the transition between the lower to upper registers, often referred to as "the break"
■ To develop muscle coordination for a seamless register transition

Origin of Exercise

Based on straw phonation theory and exercises described by Dr. Ingo Titze.

Overview of Exercise

This exercise is designed to reduce both physical strain and mental anxiety in the transition between the lower and upper registers (the terms "lower" and "upper" register are used here to avoid confusion that often comes with registration terminology). It is meant for both male and female singers who do everything in their power to avoid this transition. The basic gesture is a pitch glide between registers with an emphasis on spending time directly in the transition (the "break") as opposed to avoiding this area. The glide can be done using three different vocal tract configurations to aid in exploration and balancing: (1) straw phonation, (2) semioccluded vocal tract positions, and (3) open vowels. There are three phases to the exercise: exploration, adjustment, and smoothing. Depending on the singer, it may take several days or even weeks to move from one phase to the next.

Exercise

The key to successfully navigating the transition between the registers is to balance the laryngeal musculature (thyroarytenoid and cricothyroid muscles) while providing the minimum necessary amount of subglottal pressure. Oftentimes the transition is unsuccessful ("breaking" or "cracking") because of excessive laryngeal tension and/or subglottal pressure. This tension frequently stems from avoidance or fear of this part of the voice. Each of the three phases may be attempted with different degrees of vocal tract resistance, as detailed below.

Phase I: Exploration and Acceptance of the Transition

■ Begin on a comfortable note in the middle of your lower register ("chest voice").
■ Slide up in pitch on a mezzo piano dynamic until you reach the upper limit of your modal register and you feel the voice becoming unstable.
■ Continue sliding up in pitch until you are through the transition and are now completely in your upper register.

Phase II: Adjustment of Transition Location

■ Once you accept and are comfortable with the instability in phase I, try to adjust where the instability occurs within your range.
■ As you slide upward, take the lower register higher so that the instability begins at a higher pitch then it normally would. Warning: Never strain or push

Instead of avoiding this area of instability, spend time in this area while allowing the voice to flip between registers, like a yodel. Don't try to control your voice; instead, be a passive observer. Exploration and acceptance of breaking and cracking will help you develop the awareness and acceptance of breaking and cracking will help you develop the awareness and motor control needed to eventually smoothly transition in this area of the voice-consider this like the necessary phase of learning to ride a bike wherein you wobble and sometimes fall until you learn the right coordination and motor patterns to stabilize and ride easily.

your voice into this area. Instead, lighten up as you bring the lower register higher.

- Do the opposite on the slide downward from your upper to lower register: bring the upper register lower than you normally would.
- On the next upward slide, begin transitioning at a lower pitch than normal.
- Again, do the opposite on the downward slide, beginning the transition to the lower register at a higher pitch than you normally would.
- Continue this adjustment phase until you start to feel that you have some control over where and when the transition occurs.

Phase III: Smoothing the Transition

- Now that you have achieved some control over the transition, attempt to slide from low to high while gently shifting from one register to the next. Again, do not strain or force your voice, but lighten the sound and gently shift between registers.
- Do the same going from high to low.
- With this approach, you will not only be able to smoothly transition between registers, but you will be able to sing in a mixed voice right in the register transition that you once avoided!
- If needed, replenish your breath before sliding downward in pitch.
- As you slide downward, pay attention to when your voice begins to feel unstable. Again, as was done

on the way up, do not avoid the instability—spend time in the transition, allow it to flip back and forth.
- Eventually arrive in the lower register.
- The goal of this first phase is to embrace the instability and release the fear of cracking.

Vocal Tract Configurations

The three different vocal tract configurations below provide different degrees of resistance (vocal tract inertance). Increased inertance aids with smoothing the register transition. Each of these configurations can be used to provide varying degrees of assistance or challenge during each phase of the exercise.

Semi-occluded Vocal Tract Using Straw Phonation

Phonating through a straw provides the greatest amount of resistance, and therefore, the greatest amount of assistance. Place a straw between your lips as if you're about to sip a beverage. You may need to experiment with different diameters and/or lengths of straws to find one that is comfortable. Narrow diameter straws, such as a cocktail straw, provide the greatest amount of resistance. However, if you tend to use a lot of pressure when you sing, you may need to start with a larger diameter to reduce the resistance (drinking straw or larger). As you sing with the straw, be sure all your air is exiting the straw and is not leaking out around the straw or through your nose.

Semi-occluded Vocal Tract Using Closed Vowels

Using vowels such as /u/ or /i/ with extended lips or consonants such as /v/ or /z/ provides a resistance near the front of the mouth, similar to the straw but to a lesser extent.

Open Vowels

Open vowels, such as /a/, provide the least vocal tract resistance and, therefore, are often the hardest vowels to use during the register transition. Do not attempt this exercise on an open vowel until you are comfortable using one of the two vocal tract configurations described above.

Honking

Sarah L. Schneider

Purpose of Exercise

■ To coordinate respiration, phonation, and resonance without strain
■ To find balanced resonance to achieve a "mixed belt" voice with maximal output and minimal effort
■ To exaggerate nasal resonance during "nose pinch"
■ To find more balanced oral-nasal resonance after releasing the "nose pinch"

Origin of Exercise

I first observed this exercise in the singing studio of Margaret Baroody when she used "honking" to exaggerate sensations of nasal resonance to then achieve more balanced resonance in a sung sound. With our knowledge of resonant voice production (phonatory configuration prior to the onset of phonation) and belt voice production, while highly debated, I began using a variation of this exercise with assorted patients during vocal rehabilitation. I found specific success using this exercise to help musical theater and some commercial music singers achieve a mixed belt with less effort (theoretically less vocal impact), while allowing for the desired sound to be achieved.

Overview of Exercise

This exercise is completed in four steps beginning with reinforcing the basic building blocks of voice production—coordination of respiration, phonation, and resonance. Initially, during speaking voice production, the nose is pinched to achieve the honking sound. This sound should have exaggerated nasal resonance (pingy and "annoying"). Honking is then completed during sung sounds beginning in the middle voice, working upward in pitch and then back down as the second step. Focus is on maintaining the exaggerated nasal sensation and a sense of airflow on the hand with relatively low pressure in the throat. The third step is to begin fading the use of honking by

alternating the nose pinch and release. The patient works to maintain the sense of nasal energy—however, without the nasality of the sound. The final step, once consistency has been established, is to begin to integrate this technique into repertoire. Generally, this is integrated by singing while honking and beginning to release the nose while maintaining resonant energy but not hypernasality.

Exercise

Step 1. Honking during Speaking Voice Production

1. Pinch the nose.
2. Inhale through the mouth with an open throat and relaxed tongue, feeling expansion in the rib cage and lower abdomen.
3. During exhalation, feel a small amount of consistent warm air on the hand, while saying /nananananа/ in a comfortable speaking pitch in descending glide fashion. Feel the sound in the nose, buzzing or resonating, where the fingers pinch the nose.
4. Repeat honking several times varying the vowel. Continue to energy of sound in the nose and a small amount of consistent airflow on the hand. Experiment with pitch variation.
   a. /ninininini/
   b. /nonononono/
   c. /nainainainai/
   d. /nunununununu/

Step 2. Honking during Scales

1. Pinch the nose.
2. Inhale through the mouth with an open throat and relaxed tongue, feeling expansion in the rib cage and lower abdomen—vary the length and volume of the inhalation to suit the duration of the upcoming vocal utterance.
3. During exhalation, continue to feel a small amount of consistent warm air on the hand, while singing /nanananana/ on the scale pattern 54321.
   a. This should begin in a comfortable middle pitch range, depending on the voice classification—for example, G4 for women and G3 for men.
   b. Complete this exercise moving up a semitone at a time and then working back down through the

vocal range in the same fashion. Target specific areas that are unstable, lose nasal resonance, or become strained.

   c. Continue to feel the sound in the nose, buzzing or resonating, where the fingers pinch the nose. Feel a small amount of consistent warm air on the hand. Work to balance voice production with minimal effort and maximal nasal output.

4. Repeat honking on a different vowel and note combinations depending on the requirements of the singer.

5. Cues may be provided to release the jaw, releasing the tongue or lifting the palate to achieve and maintain the desired sound.

Step 3. Alternating Use of Honking

1. Pinch the nose.

2. Inhale through the mouth with an open throat and relaxed tongue feeling expansion in the rib cage and lower abdomen—vary the length and volume of the inhalation to suit the duration of the upcoming vocal utterance.

3. During exhalation, continue to feel a small amount of consistent warm air on the hand, while singing / nanananana/ on the scale pattern 54321.

4. Complete the same pattern /nanananana/ 54321 with the nose released.

   a. Continue to feel forward resonant energy but without hypernasality.

   b. Complete this exercise in the same manner as step 2.

   c. Work to complete the honking and released pattern on one breath.

5. Cues may be provided to release the jaw, releasing the tongue or lift the palate to achieve and maintain the desired sound.

Step 4. Integrating Sensations of Honking into Repertoire

1. Complete honking, as in the steps above.

   a. The /nanananana/ may be used to establish the desired sensation.

   b. However, you may choose to move directly to lyrics of the chosen song while honking on the melody.

2. Once the desired sensation and sound are established with honking, begin to release the nose, working to maintain resonance energy without hypernasality.

3. This can be done by singing a phrase while honking and then singing the same phrase released or by singing a phrase while honking and then releasing for the next phrase.

4. As consistency improves, sing the melody and lyrics with the nose released and intermittently use a nose pitch to check in regarding maintenance of the sensations and sound while honking (Figure 7–2).

Meow Mix

Kelly M. Holst

Purpose of Exercise

■ To encourage relaxation of the laryngopharynx
■ To develop a seamless transition from thyroarytenoid dominant to cricothyroid dominant singing

Origin of Exercise

I created this exercise to help female vocalists navigate the transition between chest voice and head voice. It is based on the principle that the voice works seamlessly, efficiently, and freely when the resonators and the action of the thyroarytenoid and cricothyroid muscles are balanced through "cross-training." I first created the "meow mix" portion of the exercise to help female singers feel the connection between energized, forward speech and "mixed" singing. The head-voice glide was added to help balance the resonators and release constriction of the vocal tract after some singers struggled with hypernasality in the meow mix.

Overview of Exercise

This exercise is for female singers of all voice types. The range utilized will depend on the voice type of the singer, but should fall between G3 at the lowest point in the meow mix and Eflat 5 at the highest point in the head-voice glide. This exercise works well early

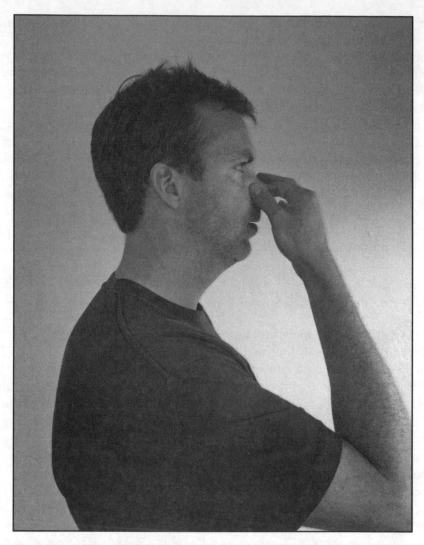

Figure 7–2. Honking. Photograph courtesy of Todd Schneider.

in a singer's warm-up cycle as it utilizes energized speech and easy head-voice glides, allowing for a gentle stretching and contracting of the thyroarytenoid muscle.

The exercise includes two parts: the descending meow mix and the ascending head-voice glide on [u][a][u]. It is extremely beneficial for women that struggle with the lower passaggio and for singers who push the chest voice in contemporary styles and experience a dramatic shift in color, quality, and power at the break. Singers with a hypernasal mix or belt will benefit by maintaining the space and height of the head-voice glide when singing the meow mix. Those who fail to energize their head voice but are confident

in their lower register benefit by retaining the energy and body connection of the meow mix when transitioning to the head-voice glide.

Exercise

Begin the exercise by speaking "meow, meow, meow, meow" with adequate breath flow and energy. The spoken "meow" should be inflected up and down, navigating from chest voice to head voice until you feel the sensation of speaking with a buzz toward the nose and teeth with absolutely no sensation of pressure or strain in the throat. Do not proceed to sing until speaking the exercise in this manner has been mastered. You will use this spoken "meow" to guide you in the meow mix portion of the exercise.

Start the exercise at D4 or E4. Begin by speaking and then singing. Execute the spoken "meow," breathe, and then sing the exercise on the descending pattern trying to match the sung "meow" to the feeling of the spoken "meow." Breathe again and do an energized head-voice glide on [u]. This should feel like a siren. It does not need to be too high, but it must start and end in your head voice. Breathe and sing the ascending do-sol-do (1-5-1) pattern on [u][a][u], starting and ending in your head voice just as you did with the siren. Both the siren and the sung glide should be very legato. An audible scoop is acceptable, if needed. It is essential that the starting pitch for the meow mix and the starting pitch for the do-sol-do glide are the same. This starting pitch serves as a pivot point that helps build kinesthetic awareness and a smooth transition between mixed and head voice production.

Fix It in the Mix

Starr Cookman

Purpose of Exercise

■ To prevent either pressed or breathy phonation through use of mix register
■ To encourage a reduction of obvious passaggio transitions

Origin of Exercise

Oftentimes, the "vocal break" is the bane of a singer's existence. This break typically occurs when a singer is shifting between modal and loft (chest and head) registers. I've found through work with both injured and noninjured singers that the use of the slow glissando through the passaggio can balance the laryngeal mechanism such that overt aphonic or pitch breaks are ameliorated. This exercise can also address the breathy/thin vocal quality often occurring due to a disadvantageous low-range extension of loft (head)

register as well as the strained/pressed quality of the disadvantageous high-range extension of chest (modal) register. This exercise uses a combination of the glissando from Dr. Joe Stemple's Vocal Function Exercises, semi-occluded vocal tract from Dr. Ingo Titze's work, the inverted megaphone vocal tract shape from Arthur Lessac, a wonderful explanation of mix register from Dr. Linda Carroll, and the concept of body-cover control of the true vocal folds from the Estill Voice Training method.

Overview of Exercise

This exercise is best used after a basic vocal warm-up involving body release/stretch and alignment, breath activation, and light vocalization, usually using a lip trill or tongue trill throughout the range. The ease of this exercise and the rapidity with which smooth transitions are acquired varies greatly from singer to singer. It is preceded by an explanation of vocal registers as a function of a coordinated effort between breath, vocal fold tension/thickness, and resonance. An emphasis is placed on vocal fold lengthening during pitch elevation. As the vocal folds lengthen, the vibrating portion of the vocal fold correspondingly migrates from "thick" to "thin." In other words, modal register typically corresponds with vibration of the majority of the vocal fold, whereas head voice and falsetto typically correspond with vibration of only the upper lip of the vocal folds. The key to a smooth passaggio is to allow for a gradual "lightening" of the vocal fold edge while elevating pitch, and conversely a gradual "thickening" of the vocal fold edge while decreasing pitch. This change in vocal fold vibrating mass and tension is achieved through a coordinated effort primarily between the cricothyroid muscles and the thyroarytenoid muscles.

Mix register is discussed as a combination of "chest" and "head" voice. Any combination is fair game on any note to produce the timbre or color desired. Some combinations (i.e., 90% chest, 10% head on a high note, corresponding with forced vocal fold thickness, pressed voice quality, and high volume) may lead to vocal fatigue and injury. In general, we want to promote a mix register composed of decreased chest voice and increased head voice for notes above the passaggio. The converse is true for notes below the passaggio. The passaggio will most likely be managed with a near 50/50 blend of registers. To experience a gradual change to and from registers by way of the concept of vocal fold thickness, glissandos are produced, first in one-octave spans, ascending to descending, all in comfortable modal register. The starting note then increases chromatically until the glissando spans modal, mix, and head voice register. Once this is completed without obvious register breaks, the one-octave span is expanded to two, then the vowel is changed from /u/ to /i/ then /a/. Finally, the glissando is produced at soft, medium, and loud volume. I've found that the /u/ glide, once mastered, often facilitates improved vocal control and confidence. Appropriate register use can reduce tension and vocal fold pressing, thereby reducing the likelihood of injury.

Exercise

Part I. Basic Glissando

1. Establish a one-octave span, easily produced primarily in modal (chest) register (suggested range for females F3 to F4; males A2 to A3).
2. After a full, abdominal release inhalation, phonate on a /u/ vowel at medium volume in an ascending, slow, gradual glissando, followed by a descending, slow, gradual glissando. Vocal tract shape is "neutral" for the lowest pitch, assuming an "inverted megaphone" shape for middle notes by gradually increasing your posterior oral space, keeping the lips in a firm /u/ position. While descending pitch, vocal tract shape gradually returns to a neutral position.
3. Vocal resonance is produced as a column along the front of the face throughout the entire glissando; back of neck, shoulders, jaw, and tongue are free from tension.

> Inverted megaphone shape refers to a vocal tract shape, where the mouth is narrow (mouth of the megaphone) relative to the posterior pharyngeal area, which is wide (open end of the megaphone).

4. Visualize the edge of the vocal fold lightening gradually with a gradual increase in pitch followed by a gradual thickening of the vocal fold edge with a gradual decrease in pitch.

Part II. Increasing Pitch

1. Once the basic glissando is produced without obvious register breaks, increase the starting note by one half step. Continue to keep alignment free from tension and breath ample. Follow vocal tract shape guidelines of assuming an inverted megaphone shape through the middle voice. Once approaching an upper range (typically D4 and above for males, C5 and above for females), allow your lips to open gradually. Continue to visualize vocal fold thickness changing with pitch.
2. Most likely, you may find a difficult span of a few notes marking a register transition for you. This is where your vocal folds want to abruptly change from thick to thin (ascending pitch) or thin to thick (descending). If you are having a difficult time achieving a smooth transition, try a descending glissando first as you might find it easier to gradually release the vocal folds into thickness rather than to gradually engage them.
3. Repeat the glissando several times in a row, slowing down around the passaggio to allow for your laryngeal muscles to work out the balancing they need to achieve a smooth transition. Remember that avoiding an abrupt break oftentimes requires releasing out of pure chest voice earlier in the ascending glissando, recruiting a mix of head voice and chest. On the way down, the break can be avoided by gradually recruiting more chest voice in your mix above and in anticipation of the passaggio. Be patient with yourself. This step may require a week or two of daily repetition.

Part II. Beyond the Basic

1. Once you can produce the one-octave /u/ glissando smoothly throughout your range, it is time to increase the difficulty of the exercise. Start by completing the same glissando spanning two octaves rather than one. Remember to keep it slow and con-

trolled. Monitor for tension and avoid phonating at the end of your breath, which can cause vocal fold pressing and strain.

2. Now it's time to change the vowel. Next, produce one-octave glissandos on an /i/ vowel. Once those are smooth, move to an /a/. Remember to maintain forward resonance throughout each glissando. Chances are, the /a/ will challenge you the most.

3. Last, produce glissandos on all vowels at soft and loud volumes. When you change the dynamics, you will also need to change the "recipe" for your mix register at particular notes. For example, for soft vocalization, head voice (thin vocal fold vibration) can predominate at lower pitches without vocal instability. For loud volume, chest voice (thick vocal fold vibration) can predominate in the mix at higher pitches.

Slidy aa's

Lisa Popeil

Purpose of Exercise

- To encourage sensation of forward pull of hyoid bone, "laryngeal lean"
- To stabilize laryngeal height on ascent of pitch
- To promote stretching and thinning of vocal fold for high chest voice

Origin of Exercise

I created this exercise in the early 1990s using the observation of "belter's bite" in professional rock, R&B, and musical theater belters. The use of sliding pitch was based on sirens, the difference being the double action of "laryngeal lean" pulling forward simultaneously as the sensation of backward pulling of the vocal folds in the stretching action of pitch ascension while remaining in chest voice.

Overview of Exercise

The "Slidy aa's" can be used by males or females in any vocal range, although its main usefulness is to help train singers to safely take a chest voice sound high in the vocal range. The goal is to take the exercise as high as possible, even to the highest note of the singer's absolute range (excluding whistle). Females can begin the 1515151 pattern on C4, and males can begin the pattern on D3, both moving up from there. Females may find that it is not exceedingly difficult to take the exercise to at least a C6. Males often find it impossible to continue to the highest note of absolute range without shifting into head voice/falsetto.

This exercise should be done after a few minutes of light warm-up as it can be challenging and only appropriate for an advanced singer. It requires strong abdominal support to avoid vocal fold pressing and laryngeal overlifting.

Exercise

Step-by-Step Instruction on How to Complete the Exercise

1. Be simple but very specific, including all relevant information (note range, dynamic range, staccato legato, etc.).

2. Start with tall posture, firmed jaw with slightly protruded chin, and head tilted up slightly. Tongue should be relaxed, tip touching gently against the bottom teeth.

3. The first note should start cleanly on the vowel "aa" (as in "cat") without a breathy onset. A click onset is allowed and can be useful. A medium to loud volume should be used.

4. Try to maintain a steady volume from low note to the fifth above and back down again. Slide the pitches up and down with no separate articulation between notes.

5. Attempt to "feel" the vocal fold stretching backward while "feeling" the upper neck pull forward, both actions and sensations as the pitch raises. This can be thought of as a "double-stretch" sensation.

6. Larynx should stay somewhat stable during the exercise, without noticeable up and down height changes.

7. Increase upper belly (below sternum) support, pushing the area out and maintaining the outward pressure steadily for the entire phrase. The lower belly (navel and below) should gradually clutch in for the entire phrase. Higher pitches will require more lower belly "in" support.

8. As the pitch rises to the highest part of the vocal range (starting on approximately Bb4 for females or A3 for males), gently push the chin down to help anchor the larynx.

Hoot-n-Holler

James Curtis and Brian E. Petty

Purpose of Exercise

■ To coordinate a clear, resonant, and easy voice for the chest, belt, and head voice registers

■ To coordinate pitch variation independent of changes with loudness and respiratory drive

Origin of Exercise

This is inspired by two different exercises learned from speech pathologist/singing voice specialist Sarah Schneider (UCSF Voice and Swallowing Center) and voice teacher Tom Baresel (University of Cincinnati—College Conservatory of Music). Based on the theories of voice science, acoustics, and principles of voice therapy, this is used to maximize acoustic output of the CCM harmonics while minimizing laryngeal strain and effort.

Overview of Exercise

This is a three-part singing exercise targeting an easy and resonant voice, deliberate changes in registers, and pitch-volume change independence. The exercise begins by cueing for a "hooty" sound. The light and "hooty" head voice helps to facilitate forward resonance, a relaxed laryngeal posture, and reduced potential for large inhalations, which lower the larynx and darken the sound (typical for classical music, not for CCM). The descending glide carries this easy and resonant voice quality into the lower registers, while also training extension of register ranges. Flipping abruptly to chest and belt voice with the twangy /ñæ/ helps to maintain the previously established concepts of resonance and ease. Last, keeping the volume consistent during the entire exercise, increase the pitch change in isolation from changes in subglottal pressure and medial compression. The entire exercise should be done on one breath with no vibrato.

Exercise

1. Using pursed lips, sustain a "hooty" /hu/ in the upper register range (beginning just above one's upper passaggio) for 2 to 3 seconds. Cues:
   ■ Sensation of a light and effortless head voice
   ■ Sensation of forward lip buzz

2. Continue sustained /u/ into a descending octave glide. Cues:
   ■ Maintain "forward focus" and "hooty head voice" entire glide down
   ■ Keep it light and soft (i.e., do not switch to chest voice)

3. Once at the descended octave, flip to chest voice and belt a /ñæ/ on an ascending/descending 151 glide
   ■ Keep feeling of an easy voice and forward resonance

- Keep the volume consistent (i.e., do not sing more loud on the top than on the bottom)
4. Continue up chromatically and work as needed.

A Three-Part Exercise for Bright Vowels in High Tenor Voices

Billy Gollner

Purpose of Exercise

- To facilitate an ease of vocal production for high chest-dominant (TA dominant) singing at Bb4 and above.
- Using brighter vowels (a resonance strategy) to address mix register, a higher laryngeal position, and a narrower vocal tract.
- While these exercises are specifically helpful for training and conditioning high tenor voices, they are also helpful for all high belters.

Origin of Exercise

While many styles of contemporary commercial music (CCM) place extreme demands on the vocal mechanism, there has always been criticism about how high is too high and if high tenor vocalists are putting themselves at risk by singing popular repertoire. The existence and demands placed on high tenor voices actually date back hundreds of years and both classical and popular art forms have employed the use of high tenors in their works—so why is so little understood about how to train them?

In 1835, Vincenzo Bellini composed "Credeasi, misera" for his opera *I Puritani*; this piece is commonly referred to as the "infamous *I Puritani* High F" (F5). By today's standards, artists like Adam Lambert, Mykal Kilgore, and Jonah Nilsson are required to sing these pitches daily and it is our job as teachers to prepare our students for the reality of the marketplace.

As a singer, I have made a living singing CCM music that lives in the stratosphere, and as a voice teacher this is my main student-base (professional CCM singers and musical theatre performers). I have been so blessed to be mentored by Jeannette LoVetri and have had the privilege of working under her guidance for most of my teaching career. These exercises come from my work as a Somatic Voicework™ teacher; they are heavily influenced from classical vocal pedagogy, specifically the concept of *Squillo*, and from my lived experience as a high tenor.

While these are some of the exercises and approaches I use when working with high tenor voices, they are also helpful for working with belters of all voice types; the starting pitches just change based on the student's voice type.

Overview of Exercise

People often refer to resonance as a catchall term for quality of sound, and the elusive nature of the word has led to great debate amongst vocal professionals. While the source of the sound is produced at the vocal fold level, resonance refers to the specific quality of sound produced by the way the sound can be adjusted as it interacts with the vocal tract. The vocal tract comprises the various areas above the vocal folds up to the lips that interact with one another and impact the quality of a sound.

In terms of practical application to the voice, there is always interaction between one structure within the vocal mechanism and all other parts. As a result, brighter vowels interact with registration, laryngeal position, and vocal tract width. When training high tenors for CCM repertoire, the vowels must skew much brighter than they would in classical vocal pedagogy.

Posture and Physicality

This is the Olympics of singing! A singer must have an established habit of excellent posture and alignment before attempting any extremes with the voice.

Unlike classical vocal pedagogy, training high tenor voices for CCM repertoire requires tenors to tilt their chin upwards. This allows for the larynx to comfortably move between high and low positions as singers reach the extremes of their range. They should

EXERCISE #2: Arpeggios on [ε] or [ae].

EXERCISE #3: Nine-Tone Scale on [ε] or [ae].

make sure their chin is slightly elevated. Tenors will want to induce a large smile, showing the top teeth.

Exercise

Part 1: Finding Bright Vowels

Begin by having the student explore a really nasty bright sound. I find using the word "ew" or "gross" can be helpful. It can also be helpful to encourage students to "put the sound in their nose." Afterwards, I always explain that the sound is not really in their nose or nasal. However, many students feel the sound resonates behind their nose, so the sensation of singing in our nose can be helpful.

When making a truly bright vowel, if students plug their nose, there will be no change in the sound. Students must go towards a much brighter sound than they would normally make in speech or singing. I encourage the students to sing with overly bright vowels at the beginning, with the initial aim being ease of vocal production rather than quality of sound (which comes with time and facility).

Part 2: Arpeggios on [ε] or [ae].

Once a bright vowel has been established, begin exploring that sound on an octave arpeggio. It is important to not go beyond what the singer can do without extreme effort; pay attention to the vowel and pitch;

when either begins to migrate, start working your way back down. Begin around F3 and work your way up and down by semi-tone. Encourage the singer to keep the sound in a very bright and whiny place.

Part 3: Nine-Tone Scale on [ε] or [ae].

Once a singer has started to achieve facility with working bright vowels, begin working the singer on a nine-tone scale. As the singer ascends in pitch, the vowel will need to get brighter. Begin around E3 and work your way up. If the singer is not bright enough at the passaggio (around F4), the ability to sing above this break in repertoire will be very difficult.

Belt Tactics: Physical Cues for Success

Ann Evans Watson

Purpose of Exercises

- To create a "bright and brassy" belt sound with an appropriate amount of air pressure, vocal fold engagement, and laryngeal ease
- To differentiate between belt registrations by using physical "cues"

- To promote ease and efficiency in the belt sound/technique
- To provide psycho-physical intentions combined with natural law and acoustics to create belt sounds that are healthy, sustainable, and repeatable

Origin of Exercises

This exercise was inspired by Robert Edwin's development of the belt voice as the "calling voice," Andrew Byrne's visual tactics for singing, and Dr. Alfred A. Tomatis, MD.

Overview of Exercises

The root principle of these exercises is that by using a combination of mental intention, visualizations, and physical gestures, as well as voiced plosive consonants and high tongue vowels, the singer can create contemporary belt sounds with appropriate amounts of both energy and ease. By using images, gestures, and high tongue vowels, the student removes the natural tendency towards pushing more TA (thyroarytenoid)/chest activation as pitch rises. This happens because the student is not thinking about the balance of head/chest in vocal production and has been given actions or "cues" that promote a shifting balance towards head voice while maintaining a chest voice dominance. This maintains the integrity of the belt sound without a static set-up. The goal is engagement and energy rather than the oft-used squeeze and tension in the vocal apparatus.

The Direct/Pop-fly/Fountain physical cues are to be used in sequence: **Direct** for lower belt which is closest to speech registration, **Pop-fly** for a student's passaggio, and **Fountain** just above the passaggio. Both the Direct and Pop-fly will employ thicker vocal folds. Fountain uses a thinner fold and may narrow the aryepiglottic sphincter (AES) and possibly aids in retracting the false vocal folds (FVFs). The exercises may also build by starting with a fricative voiced consonant sound ("v," "z") followed by an ε ("Eh"), with the next level using plosive sounds ("b," "d") and possibly more open vowels. As these tactics are employed sequentially and pitch rises, the perception of the listener is that the sounds are all of equal value. The perception of students is that of increasing ease—this to the point that they frequently can't believe that the quality sounds the same throughout because "it feels so easy."

Exercises

Before initiating the steps below, do several mid-range scales to determine the student's upper passaggio (P2).

Direct

1. Use the phrase "Hey, that's my pizza" or something similar to get the attention of someone across the street, as in a calling sound. This should produce full, bright, bodily engaged sounds that are mid-range, lacking in strain or vocal fry. *(Audio 1A & 2A)*
2. Coach the student to notice stance (grounded), head/neck position (tall versus thrust with some engagement of the sternocleidomastoids [SCM] and temporalis) and an open throated, yet highly engaged sound. Have the student repeat the phrase and notice that minimal breath effort is required, and that depth and amount happened naturally. Use these techniques to set up the body prior to singing.
3. In a 5-1 (Sol-Do) descending pattern beginning at F#4 for females and D4 for males, use the consonant "v" or "z," depending on what is most suitable for the student, with "ε" ("veh") to call as in #1. It is helpful to have the student focus on something out a window or in a corner of the room. That becomes the student's target (Figure 7–3). *(Audio 1B & 2B)*
4. As long as breath, body, and sound remain engaged and adhering to the calling circumstances/tactics, continue up in pitch by half steps. *(Audio 1C & 2C)*
5. When ease is no longer achievable with the above tactics, usually just below Passaggio 2, stop and transition to Pop-fly.

Pop-fly

1. Coach the student to review breath and physical tactics used in the Direct belt.
2. Using the same 5-1 descending pattern, switch the consonant to a "b" or a "d," depending on what is most suitable for the student. This allows for a "launch" to the sound, keeping the energy in the

Figure 7–3. Direct.

body and the front of the mouth while keeping engagement centered and out of the throat.

3. Have the student imagine that the sound is on a trajectory similar to a Pop-fly in baseball. The target is still the same. Encourage the student to use a gesture with the arch of a Pop-fly (Figure 7–4).

4. Coach the student to explore the use of the physical gesture and how it ends. If the lower pitch lacks brightness and energy, has the gesture ended below the waist in a lackluster manner? Have the eyes followed the gesture down rather than keeping on the target? Make adjustments as necessary and continue. *(Audio 1D & 2D)*

5. As long as breath, body, and sound remain engaged and adhering to the calling circumstances and Pop-fly tactics, continue up in pitch by half steps.

6. When ease is no longer achievable with the above tactics (usually only several half steps), stop and transition to Fountain.

Fountain

1. Coach the student to review the breath (less) and the physical tactics/energy (more) used in the Pop-fly belt.

2. Using the same 5-1 descending pattern, continue to use the consonant "b" or a "d," whatever is most suitable for the student. If the sound is squeezed and tight, or carries too much energy, have the student return to a fricative consonant.

3. Coach the student to imagine that the sound is now on a trajectory similar to a fountain—a big fountain in a park (I always imagine the fountains at the Bellagio in Las Vegas) rather than a drinking fountain. The target is still the same, but now the trajectory has widened to include peripheral vision. Have the student use a gesture with the arch of a fountain, starting with hands at shoulder height moving diagonally away from the body with palms down

Pop-fly

Figure 7–4. Pop-fly.

(Figure 7-5) while maintaining the calling energy (Figure 7-6).

4. Coach the student to explore the use of the physical gesture and how it ends. Encourage the student to activate peripheral vision and notice how it affects the ease and energy of the sound. Make adjustments as necessary and continue. Adjustments often include a change of stance to one foot slightly behind the other and weight slightly back to allow for more groundedness. At this point more of the head/neck muscles will be activated in lengthening. *(Audio 1E & 2E)*

5. As long as breath, body, and sound remain engaged and adhering to the calling circumstances and Fountain tactics, continue up in pitch by half steps. Coach the student to identify how the sound feels.

6. When the sound is no longer viable or becomes significantly head dominant to the teacher's ear, stop.

For most students this is several steps above where Fountain began.

7. This can be tested/explored in the passaggio by trying both Pop-fly and Fountain on the same pitch. *(Audio 1F & 2F)*

8. Coach the student to describe the feeling of the sounds as well as her/his/their perception of the sound and how it changed, particularly during this phase of the work. Most often, the Fountain exercise will feel "easier" than Pop-fly. The sensation of the sound is often as if it's resonating somewhere in front of the student.

Variations

1. It can be valuable to adjust consonant/vowel combinations to explore the energetic/bright-dark continuum. This allows for style variances, age, and

Figure 7–5. Diagonal gesture.

Figure 7–6. Fountain.

experience, and what is most conducive to the balance of energy and ease for a given student. As the student becomes familiar with the tactics, opening up the vowel is the logical progression of difficulty.

2. Change the pitch pattern to 3-5-1 (Mi-Sol-Do) to increase the level of difficulty. Coach the student to use the circumstances of 5/Sol on 3/Mi.

The Three Birds

David Harris and Laurel Irene

Purpose of Exercise

■ To explore F1 resonant strategies of whoop, hey, and acoustic mix

■ To allow body and mind to engage in free, fun exploration

■ To influence vocal fold vibration through measured acoustic resonant strategies

■ To create broad-brush mental and physical resonant strategy templates that can inspire further, fine-tuned exploration

Origin of Exercise

This game was created by David Harris and Laurel Irene of VoiceScienceWorks.

Overview of Exercise

This game is wonderful for helping people explore CCM resonant strategies and a wide range of vocal colors with little effort. The first formant can be understood as the lowest, and the strongest energy boost of the vocal tract. This energy boost plays a significant role in overall vocal tone color. This energy boost is influenced by the air contained in the entire vocal tract, though people often associate it primarily with the throat. The harmonics that this energy boost excites become among the loudest in the vocal signature, making them influential over the tone color.

Borrowing from the resonant strategy classifications of Kenneth W. Bozeman, we have expanded to include three primary F1 resonant strategies. We label them "hey," "whoop," and "acoustic mix." Calling "hey" and "whooping" shape the vocal tract in ways that create volume and stability by aligning the first formant energy boost with a specific harmonic. Though they feel and sound very different to one another, they share this distinction. Try saying "hey" loudly, or "whoohoo!" to feel the effect. The "whoop" resonant strategy aligns the first formant energy boost with the first harmonic. The "hey" resonant strategy aligns the first formant energy boost with the second-tenth harmonics, though most typically with the second-fifth. The "acoustic mix" resonant strategy differs in that it aligns the first formant energy boost between two harmonics, most typically the first and second, or second and third, though it's possible between higher harmonics as well. Importantly, each resonant strategy has influence over vocal fold coordination, vibration, and posture. Speaking simply of the amount of vocal fold muscle engagement present in phonation, a "whoop" resonant strategy is more likely to encourage the vocal folds into a ligament-dominant posture, the "hey" resonant strategy is more likely to encourage the vocal folds into a muscle-dominant posture, and the "acoustic mix" resonant strategy is more likely to encourage the vocal folds into one of myriad middle postures. As a side note, it is also possible to achieve different vocal fold postures even with a focused resonant strategy with study (e.g., a more muscle-dominant posture with a whoop resonant strategy is fairly common in many styles).

Exercise

One of our favorite games that we've created for feeling the contrast between "hey," "acoustic mix," and "whoop" is The Three Birds Game.

"Quack" like a duck, like, a really annoying duck. While quacking, flap your wings (arms) wide and run around the room if you have the space, let your inner bird fly so that you are less conscious of your voice. (Note: some people experience throat and jaw tension when being a duck. They can be more chill versions.) Let the duck go, and become a goose, slightly more sophisticated. Say "Qwaa, Qwaa, Qwaa." Tuck your hands under your armpits and waddle around (or in place if need be) "Qwaa"ing with delight.

Set the goose down, and become a pigeon. "Coooo, Coooo, Coooo"

Place one hand in a soft fist at your chest (this is the pigeon) and lightly stroke it with the other hand, being careful not to wound the pigeon as it "Cooooo"s. Play for as long as you like to enjoy the sounds. Ask your vocalists to describe the differences that they hear between the different birds, how the sounds feel different (this is where you can learn if you've got a tight duck amongst the group), and which sounds feel more aligned with their goals/norms/songs/vocal textures.

Explain to them (with the help of a voice analyzer if you can) that the pigeon "Cooo" boosts the lowest part of their sound (formant 1 energy boosts the first harmonic), that the "Quack" boosts higher parts of their sound (formant 1 energy boosts the second-tenth harmonics), and the "Qwaa" boosts several harmonics at once (formant 1 energy boosts in-between two harmonics). This will all be visibly obvious in an analyzer. They will also notice from the visual how much more overall harmonic energy is present in the "Qwaa" than the "Cooo" and in the "Quack" than the "Qwaa."

Once the sounds are familiar, begin to put them onto vocal exercises. Any vocal exercise can be used. For example, this is a five-note major scale followed by an octave glide.

Start with "Cooo" (Do, Re, Mi, Fa, Sol, Fa, Mi, Re, Do—Do—Do), then repeat with "Qwaa" and "Quack." Use the straw for added acoustic benefit.

In preparation for a song, ask students which of the three most aligns sonically with their stylistic goals. Choose that one, and sing the song as that bird (flap around if you like). For contrast, sing it as another bird and see what happens. You might discover something you didn't expect. Allow the birds to become a regular reference point for drawing ear and body into a resonant strategy sphere from which to begin to fine-tune resonant strategy goals.

References

Bozeman, K. (2013). *Practical vocal acoustics*. Pendragon Press.

Stemple, J. C., Lee, L., D'Amico, B., & Pickup, B. (1994). Efficacy of vocal function exercises as a method of improving voice production. *Journal of Voice, 8*(3), 271–278.

Titze, I. (2006). Voice training and therapy with a semi occluded vocal tract: Rational and scientific underpinnings. *Journal of Speech, Language, and Hearing Research, 9*, 448–459.

Notes

8

Vocal Styles and Specialty Populations

Bratty Twang

Norman Spivey

Purpose of Exercise

- To find a clear, forward placement
- To increase the available speech/belt range
- To find an easy, open speech/belt quality

Origin of Exercise

An exercise that mirrors speech patterns can be helpful to singers in learning to make the transition from speech to song and in developing the importance of intention in the sung monologue. This exercise uses a traditional childhood vocalism to playfully move toward a speech/belt placement and quality.

Overview of Exercise

This is an exercise I have found particularly useful with female voices. If I have a student who is unsure or self-conscious about how to proceed up the scale

toward a "belt," this playful exercise can often allow singers to successfully experiment with these sounds.

Exercise

This exercise is typically quite easy to do in the middle voice, and with encouragement can be brought right up to the top of the staff. Sometimes it is effective to encourage the student to role-play and be really bratty. Working like this tends to bring out a more carefree approach, a bolder vocalism, and additional clarity in the bright, open vowel [ae], and may even help develop strong singing actresses.

Closed Position for High Conversational Music Theater

Benjamin Czarnota

Purpose of Exercise

- To gain access to a sustainable, light chest mix while maintaining articulatory freedom

I   do owe mon-ey.   So much mon-ey!

Origin of Exercise

There are many (perhaps too many) instances in contemporary pop music theater that require actors to deliver text in a conversational manner high in their range without resorting to a head-dominant quality. Whereas more climactic moments allow for a more open position and, potentially, more leeway regarding vowel purity, these chatty moments necessitate access to a light chest mix with absolute clarity of linguistic sounds and articulatory freedom. My teacher at Indiana University, Dr. James McDonald, used an exercise he called the "Stark" exercise to access an easy, lighter "closed" position in the male passaggio. It was simply a descending major scale using the vowel sequence [u, o, a, i, u, o, a, i]. I adapted this exercise to employ an ascending leap of an octave, as well as the additional challenge presented by text delivery.

Overview of Exercise

As this exercise was devised to address a specific challenge, it should only be employed after the singer is "up and running" and before singing a piece that makes the specific demand of high, conversational text delivery with a chest dominant quality. The singer should already have access to functional chest and head registers and some understanding of how those qualities can blend.

Exercise

Begin in a mid to low range, comfortably executed in the chest (around C3 for men, A3 for women).

■ Ascend gradually by half steps, perhaps moving up and down as you go until you reach the upper

extreme that the individual can execute without constriction, understanding that the eventual goal is an upper extreme around G4-A4 for men and C5-D5 for women (these are the areas I have found to be most challenging and, again, far too prominent in contemporary pop musical theater writing).

■ The vowel I advocate for the upper "do" is closer to [dIu] than a classical [u], which seems consonant with the expectations of pop sensibilities. It requires very little lip action.

■ The goal of the first pitch is to establish a solid, open chest quality. Doing so requires that, upon the ascent, the singer must adjust the register balance, thus encouraging a wider range of motion and establishing a high level of vocal energy.

■ Attention should be paid every step along the way that no "hold" or "clench" is developing as a result of the higher jaw position—freedom is the goal!

■ As the individual descends and moves to the more open vowels, take care that the quality does not become chestier and that the volume decreases.

Woah Yeah!

Patricia M. Linhart

Purpose of Exercise

This exercise is for men or women. It stems from "excited speech." Its goal is to find the high, forward placement for pop style singing.

Origin of Exercise

This exercise is based on Stephanie Samaras' "Oh yeah." While working with students involved in 1950s musicals, I discovered how their own "excited" speech took them into a placement appropriate for the show.

Overview of Exercise

This exercise works well for both men and women, but men find it more useful in the higher tessitura and for riffing. For men and women, start in the middle voice and continue up. It should be used after a complete warm-up or even later in the session.

Exercise

Start by choosing pitches close to "excited speech." Then with great enthusiasm, speak "Woah Yeah!" Really enjoy this and feel the release of breath across the hard palette. Notice where the excited speech leaves your face! Now sing it from 1-3-2-1. Number 1 is the Woah and 3-2-1 is the Yeah. Slide from 1 to 3 and feel free to add a bit of weight from below and see how much you can safely carry to the 3rd. Feel free to fall off Yeah in the speech. Carry this as high as you feel you can do safely. The weight should decrease as you ascend the scale.

Belted "Hey"

Joan Ellison

Purpose of Exercise

- To extend belted singing range
- To learn efficient muscular coordination for belted singing
- To warm up the muscles used for belted singing and keep the muscles and tissues in condition

Origin of Exercise

I learned this exercise, or a variant, from Dr. Leon Thurman (author of *Body Mind and Voice*) when I was studying with him in Minneapolis between 1997 and 2000.

Overview of Exercise

This is one of the first exercises used for singers who are new to singing in a belt style. It's appropriate for use after 10 to 15 minutes of gradually louder, higher vocal exercises that include flute register for women and falsetto for men. It's also an effective belt warm-up for more skilled singers and can be varied to practice various popular-style singing qualities.

Exercise

Start in the lower register (around E-flat 4 for women and B-flat 4 for men), at a shouted volume level. If that is difficult, try some actual shouting on "Hey" without specific pitches first, then try to match the volume level and vocal-tract shaping while doing the pitch pattern. Singing with straight-tone (no vibrato) may be easier, as it is closer to shouting, as well as sliding up into the first pitch from a fifth lower. Repeat a half step higher, and continue as high as possible without discomfort, making appropriate adjustments to vocal tract shaping as necessary.

Typically, a soprano who has only sung Western classical-style music will feel the need to shift abruptly into the upper register around B5 (or a baritone around E4), but with appropriate mouth opening for belting and a loud enough volume level, plus muscle conditioning over time, the singer will be able to carry the belted quality higher. Skilled and conditioned higher female singers can typically perform this exercise up to around A-flat 6, and higher male singers to around C-sharp 6, with the quality becoming lighter and thinner, but still bright and brassy, as they ascend.

Belt High Notes Like Oprah Winfrey

Jennifer DeRosa

Purpose of Exercise

- To extend same ease experienced with speech-quality singing to higher pitches
- To sustain high, belted pitches once low-effort speech quality is achieved
- To reduce anxiety and constriction when belting high notes

Origin of Exercise

This exercise has been used in the context of musical theater and pop/rock repertoire to stretch speech-quality sounds typically used in low, more obtainable phrases up to pitches that are initially perceived to be above the range of speech. It is then used to show the singer how to maintain optimal resonance, ease, and a sense of call while sustaining the note for the duration of multiple beats or measures.

Encouraging the singer to imitate a familiar cultural reference allows for discovery of new vocal placement not normally associated with singing. This act of playing not only reduces effort but also reduces the pressure to sound vocally proficient within an advanced musical theater piece. The singer will simply imitate a comical sound during the exercise, but when applied to song, this sound will be appropriate to the piece and will parallel an easy and authentic musical theater high belt.

Overview of Exercise

Presuming the client has already completed a vocal warm-up, this four-part exercise begins with *Characterization: Oprah Announces the Guest*. The client will simply imitate the sound Oprah makes when announcing a guest on her show. The client then establishes the ability to effortlessly sustain or "call" a pitch within his or her speaking range in a retracted state. In the second part of the exercise, *Oprah Gives the Cue*, the client will experiment with directionality in the abstract, which, again, reduces effort needed to maximize the time the note will be suspended. In the third part of the exercise, *Oprah Gets Excited*, the client will use pitch variation to extend speech quality into the upper register. In the fourth part of the exercise, *Oprah Sings*, the client will apply this achieved sound to his or her repertoire.

Exercise

Part I. Oprah Announces the Guest—Characterization

- Enter key phrases such as "Oprah announces" and "Oprah celebrity names" into the YouTube search engine, or watch the beginning of many of the interviews Oprah facilitates. Observe Oprah Winfrey as she introduces the guests on her show. She does so with optimal false vocal fold retraction, a low effort level, and a sense of call, and she sustains one pitch for a significant amount of time. If applied to music, one would agree that she is doing what many singers desire when belting. On average, Oprah sustains a celebrity's name for about 5 seconds.
- Inhale only as much as you would when calling to a person from another room. You may find that the breath is shallow or "a chest breath," which is acceptable. Choose a celebrity you would like to have as a guest on *The Oprah Winfrey Show*. (Beyoncé is a personal favorite and consistently works well in the Oprah voice.) Announce the celebrity of your choosing to your audience using the inflection Oprah uses.

Part II. Oprah Gives the Cue—Directionality in the Abstract

- Rather than announcing your guest to your audience in front of you, consider announcing to the guest himself who is actually behind you. The guest is behind a curtain and cannot see, so he needs to hear his cue to enter the stage. Continue to sustain the guest's name for at least 5 seconds or more. Toggle between announcing the name forward to the audience and backward to the guest to establish the difference. From this point on, only announce the name to the celebrity behind you while facing forward to "the audience."

Part III. Oprah Gets Excited—Pitch Variation

■ Pretend that Oprah gets more excited to see the guest with each announcement and progressively raise the pitch each time until the desired pitch is reached (i.e., the high, suspended pitch in a song). Do not increase volume or intensity and continue to treat as spoken call rather than sung pitch. Continue to sustain the announcement for 5 seconds or longer and call backward rather than forward.

Part IV. Oprah Sings—Application

■ Finally, complete Steps I to III and then substitute the celebrity name with the lyric (word or phrase) in the song when the desired pitch is reached. For example, if the high note in the song falls on the word "alone," first announce the celebrity name, "get excited" and raise the pitch gradually with each announcement until the desired pitch is reached, and then continue to call on that pitch but insert the word "alone," as if that were now the celebrity's name. Do not increase volume, intensity, or intention. Continue to sustain the announcement for 5 seconds or longer, and call backward rather than forward.

Blissful Belting

Joan Lader

Purpose of Exercise

■ To enable musical theater performers as well as pop/rock performers to access a belt vocal quality in a healthy manner

Origin of Exercise

Jo Estill was a mentor of mine whom I met at a Julliard conference in 1982. I observed doctors, speech pathologists, and singing voice teachers belting in a master class. Jo was the first person to describe and define belting in a way that could be duplicated. Over the years, I have modeled Jo Estill's exercises and developed permutations of belting that could be applied to other genres recognizing that the demands of contemporary music require that singers access this quality to earn a living.

Overview of Exercise

Belting is generally associated with musical theater, gospel, contemporary music, and in some cases, opera. The Estill model is loud and bright, and generates great excitement. The larynx is high, the tongue is in a high position, the cricoid cartilage is tilted, the aryepiglottic sphincter (AES) is narrow, the false vocal cords are retracted, and the head, neck, and torso are anchored. This is usually used in a mid to upper range. However, it is important to warm up the voice sufficiently before attempting to belt. Belting long passages is often quite boring, and students are encouraged to layer sounds by playing around with different twang qualities leading to the climactic belt. Cooling down is essential to restore the larynx to its mid, relaxed position.

Exercise

A. Estill Model

a. Using a glottal or smooth onset on the vowel /e/, wave your arms around and imitate an Italian grandmother shouting "/eI/ Anthony" or look up to the ceiling pointing your finger and scold the neighbors upstairs "/eI/ Cut it out!" or simply cheer for your team after they've scored a touchdown and yell "Yay."

B. Permutation(s)

a. Calls (Arthur Lessac), for example, "hello," produced at different intensities, "get out of here," "places please," "go away"

b. Practicing different ways of narrowing the aryepiglottic sphincter (e.g., portraying a taunting bully [nænæ næ næ næ], singing like Alvin and the

Chipmunks, meowing like a cat, quacking like a duck, cackling like a witch, bleating like a sheep, crying like a baby)

Layla and the Canadian Surfer—Belting in Four Easy Steps

Chris York

Purpose of Exercise

■ Multistep warm-up to prepare a singer for belting by setting up anchoring, low breath volume, high tongue position, false vocal fold retraction (and semi-occlusion of the vocal tract), and twang

Origin of Exercise

These exercises are based on theories of vocal tract semi-occlusion, acoustics, and vocal physiology. The "Dude-Eh" portion was created and inspired by Estill teachers Robert Sussuma and Paul Fowler. This is my "next step" spin on their idea. Too many singers approach belting with a sense of fear and mistrust. Not knowing the proper recipes to create healthy belting sounds, they push and over-sing, thus proving the validity of their fear. The intent of this exercise set is to introduce and reinforce healthy approaches to belting. And be a bit silly about it in the process.

Overview of Exercise

This is a four-part exercise that begins with an anchoring activity to set the infra- and suprahyoid muscles. Next, the anchored singer uses a breathing and muscle isolation exercise to control retraction of the false (ventricular) vocal folds. Third, the singer speaks and calls on a middle-ranged pitch the affected words "Dude" (Düde) and "Eh!" This is then attempted in higher parts of the singer's range. Finally, the singer, setting low pressure on a highly twangy "Mmm," calls

out the word "Layla" on ascending keys. This set of vocalises should take approximately 4 minutes in its entirety and should leave the singer with a sense of healthy, very low-effort belt production applicable to male and female singers.

Exercise

Part I—Anchoring

The singer reminds the body that small muscles work best when local large muscles help them out. As vocalists, we anchor the small muscles of our larynx (attached to the hyoid bone) with the larger muscles of the head and neck (above) and the pectorals and latissimus dorsi (below). These muscles are very important to be able to engage to ensure safe belting.

Engaging the Muscles

1. To engage the pecs and lats, the singer can imagine holding on to heavy suitcases or can pull up on therapy bands that have been looped around the foot. Memorize this feeling and recall during belting.
2. To engage the head and neck muscles, including the palatal muscles, the singer can imagine gently biting into a very sour lemon wedge or eating hot pizza (palate) and eavesdropping without turning around (head and neck). Memorize this feeling to recall as well.

   Once the singer has control of these muscle groups, continue on to the next step.

Part II—False Vocal Fold Retraction

Because much of the belting process (narrow aryepiglottic sphincter—AES/twang, high tongue, possibly high larynx) invites the swallowing reflex, many new belters have a tendency to sing with constriction at the level of the false vocal fold (FVF). The singer needs to develop awareness and control of this part of the voice in order to offset this reflex.

1. While anchored, the singer takes three breaths.
   a. The first breath is an audible breath through the mouth. This is a mid FVF level and requires no effort internally.

b. The second breath is a (careful) asthmatic/stridor breath. This is FVF constriction and should be avoided at all costs.

c. The third breath is a silent breath through the mouth. The singer may feel as though "gills" are opening up. This is retraction of the FVF and should be the position used for belting.

2. Once the singer finds the retracted position, spend a while trying to keep the throat open to develop this awareness and control. Inhale and exhale, alternately, through the mouth and nose and see if the FVFs can remain retracted throughout. It may give the singer a sense of a suppressed laugh. Retraction is a major part of keeping the belt sound healthy, so spend time on this before moving on to the next step.

Part III—"Düde, Where's My Tongue, Eh?"

We want to decrease the shape of the oral cavity to help brighten the belt sound without raising the larynx too much (and thus inviting the swallowing reflex). The optimal position is a high tongue position that is narrow at the front of the mouth and open at the back (semi-occlusion). A silly word to find this position on is the surfer-affected word "Dude."

1. Practicing saying the word "Dude" in an affected tone. (Audio example provided.) Protrude and narrow the lips. Make it twangier. Add a bit of an umlaut to the vowel, almost as though saying [i] with [u] lips. Try this in several areas of the speech range. The happier your "dude" is, the better and more open it will feel at the back of the mouth/throat level.

2. After speaking your "Düde," follow it with a call on the word "Eh!" Make sure this has only a small amount of breath behind it, a very anchored soft palate, and lots of twang. The rebounded "Eh" will be in a perfect belt position. First, do it on the same pitch as "dude," then increase the pitch and call out on "Eh!"

Part IV: "Layla" (Recording Provided)

Once we've set up the belt position in the mouth and body, let's musicalize it a bit. Let the "Düde, Eh!"

position teach the mouth to say "Layla." The anchored soft palate and high tongue should be present.

1. To ensure that we don't over-blow, hum a medium pitch (the 5th of a chord, such as E major). Hold the "mmm" with the same low amount of breath needed to say "mmm-hmm," and add a ton of twang.

2. Transition from the "mmm" to the word "Lay." This should be very similar to our "Dude-Eh" position. There will be so much twang/high tongue paired with easy breath that you may start to hear overtones.

3. Singing "Lay(la)," on the 5th of your chord, jump up to the 3rd above and descend to the root (see sheet music provided). Keep anchored and your tongue high. Do not increase breath as you ascend. If tongue starts to tense, bring tip of the tongue slightly forward, just past the bottom teeth. Approach this call as one big sound, musically. Ascend in keys up into the belt range. Always start first with the "mmm" to keep breath pressure low. Watch for constriction and add more of a laugh to the sound the higher you get. Enjoy!

Boom Ba Chicka

Matthew Edwards

Purpose of Exercise

■ To loosen the anterior and posterior tongue
■ To encourage rhythmic singing
■ To emphasize the backbeat

Origin of Exercise

While living in upstate New York, I had the opportunity to work as a vocal consultant for a recording studio. I was frequently called in to help singers improve their intonation with the hope of eliminating the need for auto-tune. In many cases, technical problems were not the cause of the pitch issues. More often than not, the singers were unable to rhythmically sync their voice with the beat of the song. Many of these singers had prior voice training, and I realized that we as teachers often vocalize students melodically, but seldom rhythmically. I first learned to beat box while coaching an a cappella group as an adjunct at Hartwick College in upstate New York. This exercise draws from consonants and tongue movements found in beat boxing with the goal of training singers to begin thinking rhythmically when singing contemporary commercial music (CCM) styles.

Overview of Exercise

This exercise is best suited to the chest voice in both men and women. Use this exercise after warming up and before working on songs that are rhythmically driven. Songs where this style of singing are appropriate include "I'm yours," by Jason Mraz; "Wannabe," by Spice Girls; "Crazy," by Gnarls Barkley; and nearly every song within the hip-hop/rap genre.

Exercise

- Begin this exercise in a comfortable part of the chest voice with a tempo of approximately 105 bpm.
- Playing the octave bass notes as written will give the exercise a pop/rock feel.
- Move up the keyboard by half steps until the exercise becomes difficult, then descend by half steps. If two measures in each key are not enough, feel free to extend the exercise as long as needed.
- Try the various word combinations. Examples include boom chicka and deedle daddle. Feel free to make up others as well.
- As the singer becomes comfortable with the exercise, speed up the tempo (the upper limit is usually around 135 bpm).
- It may also be helpful to have the student step and clap with the beat. Broadway audition coach V. P. Boyle uses what he calls the "Two Four Dance" to teach students to feel the backbeat. Have the students step left with their left foot on beat one, clap to the left on beat two, step to the right on beat three, and clap to the right on beat four. As

they do the "Two Four Dance," encourage them to loosen up their entire body, especially their knees, shoulders, hips, and neck.

Phrase Shifting

Marcelle Gauvin

Purpose of Exercise

- To develop a jazz approach to song phrasing
- To deepen rhythmic connection to a song's meter and its subdivisions
- To increase song interpretation possibilities
- To develop spontaneous phrasing skills promoting improvisational ideas

Origin of Exercise

This exercise was inspired by jazz pianist/educator Barry Harris, known for his work with instrumentalists and vocalists alike. It's an approach jazz musicians each master when honing their interpretive and improvisational skills. As a student of jazz, I was amazed by the influx of new ideas that came just by learning to rhythmically displace a phrase!

Overview of Exercise

Phrasing shapes the musical conversation we have within each song. When done well, it contributes to the song's dynamic arc and message. Jazz phrasing at its most creative is spontaneous and highly improvised; inspired by the musical landscape and mood that surrounds it. This exercise attempts to break a singer's established phrasing patterns by imposing a variable starting point to a musical phrase. Through this planned rhythmic displacement, the singer learns to adjust the phrase while continuing to create a meaningful, musical statement within the exercise's structure.

Exercise

Part 1

1. Create a simple two bar phrase using scat syllables. In the first bar, use a melody line consisting only of eighth notes. The second bar consists of one whole note.
2. Begin to sing the phrase repeatedly, each time dropping an eighth note off the front end of the melody. Eventually you will be left singing only the "and" of beat four and the whole note of the second bar.
3. At that point, begin to add one eighth note back from the original melody with each repeat. You will end up reconstructing the original melody in its entirety.
4. Practice this exercise by swinging eighth notes to deepen the traditional jazz feel.

Part 2

1. Add lyrics to the eighth note phrase. Can you adjust the phrasing to get all the lyrics in by utilizing the four beats of the second bar? Can you keep your phrase musical while doing so?
2. Apply this approach to a piece of repertoire. By purposely displacing your phrasing, can you create a new approach to musical ideas that sounds natural but unlike your habitual patterns?

R&B Riff Exercise

Jeffery Evans Ramsey

Purpose of Exercise

■ To increase flexibility and agility in the voice
■ To encourage vocal freedom without assistance from jaw
■ To work on melisma in contemporary styles
■ To further encourage mixed voice with faster passages

Origin of Exercise

This exercise was inspired by the work I've been doing in my private lessons and classes, along with the work of such contemporaries as Gabrielle Goodman and Dr. Triniece Robinson, who both wrote books on contemporary singing, specifically in the context of R&B, gospel, and jazz.

Overview of Exercise

The main objective of this exercise is to help facilitate more flexibility in the voice by helping singers to understand that agility in riffs doesn't happen from moving the mouth and jaw; that everything they need to move the notes happens from an internal event, not external. One of the common misnomers growing up is that you have to contort the face in order to make sound; in other words, you have to get ugly when you sing. This same philosophy gets carried over into vocal technique, but once you know how sound is produced, those myths get debunked. This is true particularly when it comes to executing riffs of longer duration, which these days are done at a lightning fast pace with some of today's singers of gospel and R&B in particular. Range is synonymous with flexibility but it is also true for agility in one's voice, so getting the folds to lengthen and stretch is key to executing accurate runs, as they're also called from time to time. If you're trying to carry too much weight of chest in the riffs, the voice won't move as quickly. In classical music the coloratura is known for being able to do faster passages with her voice because it is light in quality. No matter the voice type, we do need to adhere to some of this, hence the thinner vocal folds as opposed to thickness, which will make the voice heavy; too heavy to do faster melisma. What is needed is indeed more of a mix. There are times you'll hear a singer in gospel execute a riff, starting in head voice, and coming all the way down an octave in chest. They can't do this without starting with thinner folds.

Exercise

1. You may want to start out with just singing the rhythm first without the melody just to get the rhythmic feel of the exercise. I recommend using a metronome and taking the exercise at a slower tempo. Start at around 80 beats per minute (bpm) (original tempo is 94 bpm).

© 2019 Jeffery Evans Ramsey

2. As you start to become more comfortable with the rhythm, add the melody. See if you can get your voice moving without the jaw. I sometimes have students put their hands on their jaw to monitor whether it's relaxed or trying to assist with the riffs. It's important to stay as relaxed as possible and let the folds do the work here. It will be hard at first but the payoff of less tension is worth it.

3. From here, you can now work on allowing the voice to move without push. That means that if within the exercise you need to change registers (from chest to mix or headier mix), give yourself permission to do so. This works better if you keep the volume level even throughout the exercise, as it will encourage the vocal folds to lengthen as we go higher.

4. Now that we've gotten the basics down, let's now see how close we can get to the original tempo. Remember, you're starting slow at first, but the goal is to get to 94 bpm, so slowly bring the metronome number up as you practice until you can sing to the accompaniment track tempo.

5. Once you've worked on this and feel comfortable with the exercise, feel free to work on an even faster tempo. You can now trust that your voice has the agility without the jaw or tongue's interference (tongue is usually not as big of a culprit in executing riffs as the jaw, but always check them both).

6. Lastly, while I've used /o/ for this example, please find which vowel works best for you and continue to experiment with all of them, as one vowel may be more challenging than another.

Multiple Personalities Vocal Exercise

Wendy D. LeBorgne

Purpose of Exercise

- To explore multiple vocal qualities through speech and vocal play
- To carry over multiple commercial vocal qualities into song

Origin of Exercise

The origin of this spoken and sung exercise stems from work in speech pathology, acoustics, singing, and dialect training. As commercial music singers are required to perform many different sound qualities within the same instrument, knowledge of acoustics of resonance tubes, combined with dialect training, and personal singing experimentation led to the development of this exercise. Intrigued by similarities and differences of the speaking voice quality of a given patient or singing client compared with the person's actual voice production inspired the development of this "multiple personalities" vocal experimentation exercise.

Overview of Exercise

This exercise uses a common song/melody appropriate to the level of singers vocal skill level (e.g., easy melody: Row, row, row your boat (stepwise intervals); moderate: Twinkle, Twinkle Little Star (increased intervals and range); Hard: Star-Spangled Banner (larger range with larger interval leaps). Using one or two lines of the text, singers will first speak (within a given style), then sing the song (within the same style). Singers are encouraged during the speaking portion of the exercise to notice breath, breath effort, larynx (height/ effort level), and likely most importantly, consonant and vowel placement and spaces. They are encouraged to notice any idiosyncrasies of their speaking patterns within a given "dialect." For this exercise to be successful, it is imperative for the teacher to be an expert listener and for vocal students to learn to internalize their body, breath, vocalizations, and resonators.

Exercise

Potential key elements for students and teachers to be aware of as they experiment with the exercise are: (1) physical stance/body position when they take on the different "personalities," (2) breath—is it high? low? shallow? deep? (3) breath effort—is this personality aggressive or gentle in her/his/their breath effort?

(4) perceptual awareness of both laryngeal movement (height adjustments) and phonatory effort for a given personality, and (5) speech markers characteristic of the personality (fry, growl, hard glottal attacks, aspirate attacks)—where do the vowels sit? How does the oral space feel? How does the pharyngeal space feel? Does the personality demand a nasal quality? Jaw? Tongue? Palate?

1. Take the first several lines of a common song that is technically appropriate for the skill level of the singer and speak in a naturally inflected pattern. As the teacher, be aware of any dialectical deviation from standard dialect. Ask students to gain an awareness of how their typical speaking voice feels within their body. ***If there are any deviant dialectical issues or deviant vocal qualities in the speaking voice, these may need to be addressed and corrected prior to moving to the next step of the exercise. The goal is to help the student find speaking "neutral."

2. Next, ask the student to overemphasize the following vocal qualities (one at a time) while speaking the same lyrics from the first time: opera singer; deep southern accent; rap star. Was it an acceptable production of the requested quality? If not, help guide the singer toward possible strategies to make the target voice quality more acceptable. Ask students to verbally describe what they hear and feel in each voice quality. Guide them to help discover how this "new voice" varies from their typical speaking voice within their breath, voice, and body.

3. Once singers have a grasp of how they are producing each of the given spoken vocal qualities with respect to breath, sound, and resonance, ask them to attempt to maintain the same strategies while singing the tune (aka sing like you speak!). Choose a comfortable key (within their speaking voice range). Assume the postural stance, breath patterns, breath energy, laryngeal adjustments, and resonance strategies for a given "personality." Use this exercise to play with the voice and explore multiple timbres and style choices.

4. End the exercise by having the students return to their vocally neutral placement by having them speak and then sing in their typical voice and timbre.

Register Isolation for Choral Singers

Edward Reisert

Purpose of Exercise

■ To enhance flexibility among different register qualities
■ To strengthen register qualities throughout the range

Origin of Exercise

This exercise is derived from Cross-Choral Training, created by Dianne Berkun-Menaker of the Brooklyn Youth Chorus. In working with choral students from a functional standpoint, students must have a deep understanding of the technical skills required to isolate registers. This is important for the authentic performance of a wide array of repertoire in a single concert program. Last, the consistency of registration among the singers will enhance balance and blend among the soprano, alto, tenor, and bass sections.

Overview of Exercise

Over the course of a warm-up with choral students, focus is placed on register isolation in head voice, chest voice, and mixed voice. Once those registers are accessed, the students are then asked to perform extended exercises that demonstrate their ability to apply those different register qualities in a single exercise. This exercise may be used in both male and female choral singers, although it is aimed at adolescent female choral singers who may have a tendency to bring chest register too high or have difficulty in isolating a pure head register.

Exercise

The musical pattern is Do-Sol-Do-Sol-Do, beginning at D4 (an octave lower for men). Each note is sung for four beats, at a moderately slow tempo.

The first note is sung in chest register [a], second note is sung in mix [o], high note is sung in pure head register [u] (or falsetto for men), then back down.

Pattern continues upward by half step to G4, and again downward to D4.

Light Chest Mix for Mixed Choir

Thomas Arduini

Purpose of Exercises

■ To access a light chest voice in all voices
■ To create blend and balance through registration

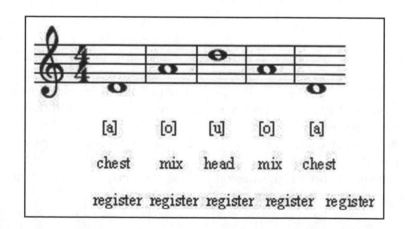

Origin of Exercises

It is important for individual choir singers to be able to functionally produce specific registration qualities individually so that they may be applied in the choral setting. When individual singers can identify and produce specific registration qualities, it allows the ensemble to widen its expressive capability and color palate. Ensembles can quickly access specific registrations for repertoire and conductors can effectively use registration to enhance interpretive aspects of performance.

Overview of Exercises

This exercise is used to access a light, relaxed, easily produced light chest register, especially in the mid to lower female and upper male range. It is most effective after a brief warm-up of slides of 3rds and 5ths. The exercise may be used to prepare to sing a piece. It can also be used to shift gears in the middle of rehearsal. It is effective for pop, madrigal and jazz styles.

Exercises

The musical pattern is Sol-Fa-Mi-Re-Do descending, beginning at A4 for all voices.

Legato quarter notes descending at a slow tempo.

Always sing softly [p]. Stay as lightly as possible, lifted palate and light production throughout.

Exercise 1

Step 1: Men (in light falsetto) sing the pattern on [u] beginning on A4. Repeat one half step higher on b flat and continue men only up to C and back to A4.

Step 2: Add the sopranos and repeat the pattern, matching the vocal quality of the men. Repeat pattern.

Step 3: Altos join at A4. Continue the pattern up to C and then continue with all.

Back down to beginning A4. Repeat entire sequence on [o] or [a]. Repeat again on [i]. Listen to each section together and individually then move on to step 2.

Exercise 2

On F3 continue all voices unison ascending 5 tone scale pattern (Do-Re-Mi-Fa-So-Fa-Mi- Re-Do) on [o] or [a] vowel at soft volume. Keep volume in check, as well as the light and lifted quality of exercise 1. Gradually increase volume to [mf], repeating the pattern until you experience a unified light chest register at moderate volume.

Sing the opening phrase of a pop, jazz, or Renaissance piece in this registration.

When the choir creates the appropriate sound, label this registration (i.e., "light jazz" or "pop") and in subsequent rehearsals recall the label to see if the group can produce the desired registration quality upon demand.

Acting Through Song: Discovering Connections to Express Ourselves Clearly as Artists

Naz Edwards

Purpose of Exercises

These exercises are designed, first, to make the artist aware that he or she is having an emotional connection with his or her art and, second, to help the artist transform those emotional feelings into movement, and thus to realize a performance with depth and clarity.

Origin of Exercises

These exercises have evolved organically over my many years of being a working actor/singer, on Broadway, on tours, and in regional theaters. I have acquired and developed them through and from my experiences with many amazing directors and teachers, and they represent part of my own path to expressing my true self as a performing artist.

Whatever our artistic craft may be, we have signed on to communicate our art so that an audience can clearly connect and join us on our journey. Above all else, we are *storytellers*. (I am using singing here, but these exercises can be adapted to work for all creative artists.)

Exercises: Connect–Create–Communicate

Part 1: Connect

Most of the time we do not realize it, but when we are choosing our material to use in performances or auditions, we have already started an emotional connection with it and ourselves. A question to ask yourself is: *Why* and *what* drove me to choose this material? This is when you remove the music from the song.

Exercise

Make a lyric sheet. This gives you a story, in the form of poetry. Read the story over and over again and see where it takes you. What words really stand out to you, what phrases trigger a reaction from you? Highlight these areas, and on another page write down the words that express these highlighted areas. Ask yourself how you feel about them. Then write down these words, and now you can see how you are feeling about the story. These are your true emotions, no one else's— yours. You've triggered a true emotional response and have identified what it is.

Part 2: Create

Now that you are aware of these emotional connections, it is time to attach an action to them and bring them to life. Here we ask ourselves: how do I react when I feel these moments?

Exercise

Write down your reactions. Now go back and read the story again, adding these reactions to the words or phrases you've chosen. It's very much like coloring your voice when singing or acting or even playing an instrument. You map out a vocal journey, and you also need to map out an emotional journey.

What emotions trigger your actions? Use those emotions to clearly communicate these actions through your art.

Part 3: Communicate

We are here to communicate with clarity the story of our art to our audiences so they can join us through the journey. When we attach an action through our art it comes alive! Even if you choose a song that has been sung a million times, it will truly be your song, because you found what it means to you, and your personal story will be felt.

Exercise

Now, bring the music back, and integrate it into your story. The music is there to enhance the story. When the story and the music truly come together, it is a magical experience, not only to the storyteller but to the audience as well.

Sing the song as if you wrote it! We hear that a lot, and it's true. By connecting with your emotions and then attaching your action to them, the songs become yours. It is so very important to know how you feel. By being in touch with ourselves and our emotions, we feed our imaginations and dreams to create incredibly imaginative art. Whether you are singing, acting, playing an instrument, or painting, you are having a relationship:

SINGERS, with your story, voice, and music

ACTORS, with your play, voice, and words

MUSICIANS, with the emotional connection between player and instrument

PAINTERS, through your colors (or perhaps lack of color), shapes, and strokes

We are all being taken on an adventure, one in which we have no idea how the ending will turn out. Really, it is none of our business. It is our business to tell our story through our imagination and our willingness to ask ourselves, "How am I feeling?"

The Ultimate Rock Sound

Sheri Sanders

Purpose of Exercise

■ To teach singers how to trust their training and invite emotions onto the voice

Origin of Exercise

This technique is based solely on an extensive study of all styles of popular music: gospel, blues, jazz, Motown, 70s folk/rock, disco, 80s pop/rock, country, contemporary pop/rock and alternative rock and punk, hip hop, and R&B, their place in society, and their relationship to musical theater. The majority of our favorite pop artists are well trained. What is affecting us the most as an audience is not their technique and placement. What affects us is the way their emotions travel on their voice.

Overview of Exercise

This exercise is very different than most exercises you will do with your voice teacher. I will invite you to leave all the great work you do with her/him/them on the "back burner" for this exercise, and then when you are through, incorporate this exercise *back* into your technique. This exercise is a complement to the work. In it you will find that it adds dynamics, flavors, colors, and textures to a healthy vocal function. So, for example: when we listen to Adele, we don't think, "To play the role of Adele, I need to think what I'd be like if I were a plus-bodied British singer who struggles with polyps and relationship issues. . . . First, I need to properly place my voice so I have Adele's quality." Instead, you would listen to ANY of Adele's albums and *feel* how the lyrics and music affect *you* emotionally. When these emotions come up in you, it creates dynamics in both your sound and personal character that can travel safely on your well-trained voice.

Exercise

Part 1: The "Setup"

Pick a lyric from your favorite pop song. Any song. Any time period. Just make sure it's a COMPLETE phrase. Since we're talking about Adele, let's use my favorite song of hers, "Rolling in the Deep," as an example:

"We could've had it all, rolling in the deep, you had my heart and soul in your hands, but you played it, you played it you played it you played it to the beat."

Sing through this piece of song FIRST with your best, well-trained technique. Properly placed. Healthy posture, with proper breath support.

Then, sing the whole phrase in your head voice, or "head-voice it."

Then, "mix it."

Finally, BELT IT OUT!

Part 2: An Emotional Experiment

In legit musical theater, we are told that having feelings, or dwelling in our feelings is self-indulgent and our focus needs to be on the other person and moving the plot. This is very fair. In singing popular music, the "character singing this song" is YOU, and it is a pure form of your emotional expression. So the "other person" needs to be taken off of the stove, and so does moving the plot. We need to think instead, if I were alone in my room and no one was looking, can I freely express how this "other person" makes me feel?? This is wonderful to bring back to our legit musical theater world so we can, ideally, create a great character with a rich emotional life who moves the plot beautifully with the rendition of their song.

Here's how you create your emotional life on popular music:

Take your lyric, again. Let's use "Rolling in the Deep" here. I would like for you to sing this phrase with the following emotions running through you:

"I love this song! It is fierce!"

"I miss you."

"Why on earth would you bail on me like that? I've been awesome to you!"

"How DARE YOU."

"You don't *deserve* to be with me. Kiss my ass."

How did the sound change with the point of view changed? Did you notice any textures, flavors, and dynamics coming through? Any noticeable differences between them?

You *should* find some really cool stuff.

And p.s. . . . when showing emotions that are strong, like "how DARE you" and "I've been awesome to you!" That doesn't mean I want you to scream. It means I want you to fill it with the "fire" and "fever pitch" that Adele sings about in "Rolling in the Deep." She's not screaming into the mike and you should not be screaming either. You should be turning up the heat on your emotions which creates power in your voice. It is very different from belting, "screlting," or screaming. Think of it like a volume dial on a radio and you are simply turning it from a 4 to a 7 or 8. Never a 10!

Again, you don't have to try this exercise on "Rolling in the Deep." If you pick a different song, please pick four or five different feelings *you* can express in THAT song. Five totally different ways to feel it. Start with joy and love, and then start letting the detailed emotions come through, one at a time.

Your feelings change the texture, colors, flavors, and dynamics of your voice, making it cooler, more interesting, more appealing and ultimately, competitive!

Verbal Diadochokinesis Exercise for Postmenopausal Women and Aging Male Voices

Barbara Fox DeMaio

Purpose of Exercise

- To help rebuild clear articulation
- To encourage the use of speech-like singing used in "musical theater legit" songs, although it can also be used for classical voice.

Origin of Exercise

I created this exercise to improve diction in my postmenopausal female students. I have also found it to be useful for older male students who have slight speech defects, such as stuttering, and for any student who needs to improve diction and create a more speech-like sound rather than what my teacher Nancy Stokes Milnes always called "the round sound" of classical singing.

Overview of Exercise

The most frequent voice-related complaints among postmenopausal women are dryness of the throat, frequent throat clearing, lower frequency levels of the voice, and voice sound alterations with increased roughness and hoarseness, as well as edema in the vocal folds. Abitbol, in his groundbreaking study of the effect of hormones on the voice, mentions dryness as one of the symptoms of the menopausal voice, and he attributes this to the loss of estrogen that occurs during menopause. Investigators in Brazil researched the vocal sound alterations reported by many women by comparing 45 in reproductive age to 45 who were postmenopausal and who were not on hormone replacement therapy for at least 3 years. The scientists found less variation in formants and verbal diadochokinesis in postmenopausal women. Verbal diadochokinesis "may be defined as the maximum speed of movement with which a given reciprocating act (such as syllable repetition, tongue protrusion, or jaw movement) can be performed without confusion in the movement." Verbal diadochokinesis and the resulting impairment of articulation can interfere with the clear diction essential to the elite singer.

Heman-Ackah, in a report on the findings of the Women's Health Initiative for the Perimenopausal Singer, says:

> *Because one of the chief functions of estrogen is to maintain the tone and bulk of skeletal muscles, including those in the larynx, many women develop atrophy of the vocal fold muscles and a reduction in the thickness of the mucosa of the vocal folds with estrogen loss during menopause.*

Hemen-Ackah also reported a perceived reduction in the mobility of the cricoarytenoid joint that can affect vocal mobility.

Menopause also affects the vagus nerve that largely innervates the larynx. Estroprogestational impregnation improves the responsiveness of the vagus nerve. However, during menopause the radical drop in the secretion of estrogens and the complete halt in the secretion of progesterone due to the lack of follicles in the ovaries have the opposite effect. The result of these neurological changes is a slowing of the vocal response and difficulty with rapid changes of frequencies when singing. This is seen in the slowing of the vibrato rate from seven to four oscillations per second that is induced by menopause.

Exercise

This exercise utilizes common tongue twisters, and can be performed on any four- or five-note exercise such as 5-4-3-2-1, but it is good to begin with only one sustained note. It has been my experience that many older women have been taught to avoid chest voice, and if that is the case, first perform the exercise in the speaking voice without any set pitch. Then begin at middle C or below, slowing raising the pitch by half steps and encouraging the singer to keep a speech-like quality, without strain.

Any tongue twister that fits the pattern you are using will work, but the best results will be obtained if you use tongue twisters that emphasize "m" and "n," and "s" or dental consonants such as "t" and "d." I like to use tongue twisters that are appropriate for the season, if possible. Any tongue twister can be used. Here are some common suggestions:

Nine nice nurses nursing nicely.

My mother makes marmalade.

Many men mention Mary.

Thirty-three thieves thrilled the throne.

Six sick hicks nick six slick bricks.

Halloween:

Dracula digs dreary dark dungeons.

Which witch wished which wicked wish.

Profession Pumpkin pickers pick the plumpest pumpkins.

Transylvanian tree trimmers are trained to trim the tallest trees.

Christmas and Hanukkah (any holiday can work):

Santa's sack sags slightly.

Silly snowmen slide and slip.

Ten tiny toy trains toot ten times.

Debbie dreaded the dreidel disaster.

Hanukkah Harry hurried home.

Minnie minded the metal menorah.

Creating the Logical 16-Bar Audition Cut

Robert Marks

Purpose of Exercise

■ To provide a template for singers to create a 16-bar audition cut

Overview of Exercise

Many of today's auditions insist that singers perform shortened versions of their songs, with 16 bars being the most common requirement. Although simply using the final 16 bars of a song will sometimes be acceptable, there are often more creative edits that will allow a singer to present a more complete-sounding song, even within the constraints of a certain number of bars. Below are some helpful tips for selecting a solid 16-bar cut.

Exercise

1. As a bar (or measure) is not a specific unit of time, often a singer will be allowed to sing approximately 45 to 40 seconds of music, regardless of the actual number of bars requested.
2. A 16-bar audition is essentially an introduction to the audition panel, determining whether a performer gets to the next round of auditions.
3. Shortened versions of songs need to show a singer off at his or her best. Be sure the "money notes" are included.

4. Cuts *must* be prepared in advance. Best to have music cut for the contingencies of either 16- or 32-bar auditions.

5. Performers should not sing from the beginning of the song and expect to be cut off. It's always best to show that the directions were followed.

6. Piano introductions must be clearly marked, even if just a bell tone. It's important to know exactly what you expect to hear from the accompanist.

7. If cuts are complicated, requiring multiple page turns and complex navigation, it's best to have a separate copy of the edited sheet music of the song, clearly marked and cut for the accompanist.

8. A good 16-bar arrangement will sound like an entire song, with a beginning, middle, and end. Avoid beginning a cut with words such as "but" and "and," which leave listeners wondering what they missed.

9. Occasionally, music of one section of a song makes more sense with lyrics from a different section.

10. Respect the musical and dramatic integrity of the song, while allowing the singer's voice, personality, and acting ability to shine.

References

Abitbol, J. (2006). *Odyssey of the voice* (p. 225). Trans. Patricia Crossley. San Diego, CA: Plural Publishing.

Abitbol, J., Abitbol, P., & Abitbol, B. (1999). Sex hormones and the female voice. *Journal of Voice, 13*(3), 431.

D'haeseleer, E., Depypere, H., Claeys, S., Borsel, J. V., & Lierde, K. V. (2009). The menopause and the female larynx, clinical aspects and therapeutic options: A literature review. *Maturitas, 64,* 30.

Heman-Ackah, Y. D. (2004). Hormone replacement therapy: Implications of the Women's Health Initiative for the Perimenopausal Singer. *Journal of Singing, 60*(5), 471.

Meurer, E., Wender, M., Corleta, H., & Capp, E. (2004). Phono-articulatory variations of women in reproductive age and postmenopausal. *Journal of Voice, 18*(3), 369.

Siarris, C. (2009). The *aging female voice: Medical treatments and pedagogical techniques for combatting the effects of aging with emphasis on menopause.* DMA thesis, University of South Carolina, p. 23.

Tuomi, S. K., & Winter, N. M. (1977). Diodochokinesis and articulation impairment. *Human Communication*, Autumn, 141.

Notes

Conclusion

The goal of this book is to provide physical, vocal, and mental exercises for working with contemporary commercial music (CCM). This includes preparation of the singer as a whole, encompassing the mental component of singing in addition to the structural components of posture, breathing, and alignment. Vocal work is broken down into segments beginning with warm-ups and cool-downs to engage and calibrate the voice prior to active technical work. The next segment provides exercises on technical voice work addressing the essential skill sets of coordination, stamina, strength, and registration. These exercises provide the basis for technically sound singers, who will eventually engage in specific high-level technical work in all vocal styles. The exercises included in this book are meant to serve as guidelines, and singers are encouraged to continue to modify and create exercises to suit specific needs with the understanding that all vocal exercises should feel comfortable even if they are challenging, and the singer should never feel vocal strain or excessive effort.